North Carolina

PORTRAIT OF THE LAND AND ITS PEOPLE
by John Rucker

CHIP HENDERSON

American Geographic Publishing

Left: *North Carolina School of the Arts in Winston-Salem.*
Below left: *Handmade musical instruments have a long tradition in North Carolina.*
Below right: *Piper at the Highland Games.*

Facing page: *Sailboaters returning at sunset.*

Title page: *Sunset along the North Carolina coastline.*

Contents page: *Enjoying the Appalachian Trail in western North Carolina.*

Front cover: *Rhododendron and Smoky Mountains.* CHIP HENDERSON PHOTO

Back cover, left: CHIP HENDERSON PHOTO.
Right: TOM TILL

American Geographic Publishing is a corporation for publishing illustrated geographic information and guides. It is not associated with American Geographical Society. It has no commercial or legal relationship to and should not be confused with any other company, society or group using the words geographic or geographical in its name or its publications.

ISBN 0-938314-63-7

Text © 1989 John Rucker
© 1989 American Geographic Publishing
P.O. Box 5630, Helena, MT 59604
(406) 443-2842

William A. Cordingley, Chairman
Rick Graetz, Publisher & CEO
Mark O. Thompson, Director of Publications
Barbara Fifer, Production Manager

Design by Linda McCray
Printed in Korea by Dong-A Printing through
    Codra Enterprises, Torrance, CA

Preface

I hope this little book will help North Carolinians and people who have made the state their home understand it better. It took me many years of living in places very far away, and a great deal of reading, before I began to understand the things I took for granted, growing up here. As T.S. Eliot once stated, "The end of all our wandering is to return to the place where we started and know it for the first time." Anyone who grew up in North Carolina heard it referred to as a "valley of humility between two mountains of conceit." There is more truth to that than one might suspect, and this book cites historic trends and events that help to explain North Carolina's identity, unique in the South.

This book is dedicated to Suzanne Evans.

J.R.
July 1989

About the Author

John Rucker is a native of North Carolina and a graduate of University of North Carolina at Chapel Hill. A former high school English teacher who taught in Montana and Alaska, later turning to commercial salmon fishing, Rucker notes that the South's oral tradition has made North Carolina a place where writers toil not so much for publication but to be read by each other and their friends: "Writing is a cottage industry in North Carolina." His book *Melancholy Bay* is a journal of his four years in Alaska.

New River

Cone Memorial Park

Blue Ridge Parkway

Stone Mountain State Park

Pilot Mountain State Park

Hanging Rock State Park

Guilford Courthouse Nat. Military Park

MOUNTAINS

Wilkesboro

Winston-Salem

Greensboro

Greensboro Hist. Museum

Durham

COASTAL PLAIN

Murfreesboro

Currituck Sound

Wright Bros. Nat. Mem.

Albemarle Sound

Raleigh Nat. Mem.

Elizabeth II Vessel

High Point

High Point Museum

Chapel Hill

North Carolina Zoological Park & Gardens

Oregon Inlet

Mt. Mitchell

Great Smoky Mountains National Park

Asheville

Biltmore Estate

PIEDMONT

Raleigh

Greenville

Pea Island Nat. Wildlife Refuge

Joyce Kilmer Memorial Forest

Blue Ridge Parkway

Chimney Rock

Lake Lure

Mint Museum of Art

Bentonville Battleground

Pamlico Sound

Cape Hatteras Nat. Seashore

Cowee Valley Mines

Charlotte

Discovery Place

Fayetteville

New Bern

Tryon Palace

TIDEWATER

Ocracoke Inlet

OUTER BANKS

N

W   E

S

Jacksonville

Fort Macon St. Park

Lumberton

Waccamaw

Wilmington

Intercoastal Waterway

USS North Carolina Battleship Mem. St. Park

Atlantic Ocean

Contents

CHIP HENDERSON

The Colony Different

Above: *A homestead in the North Carolina highlands.*

Facing page: *Rhododendron on Mt. Mitchell, North Carolina's highest point.*

In March 1969, through the window of the *Apollo 9* spacecraft from 120 miles up, Rusty Schweikart snapped a photograph of the east coast of the United States, using a hand-held Hasselblad camera with normal daylight film. The most dramatic photograph of the mission, it eclipsed all others taken automatically and using far more sophisticated films. Schweikart's photograph captured a physical feature unique on the earth. There lay North Carolina's Outer Banks, sweeping down from Virginia in a series of graceful, thin, silver arcs, and sickle-pointed capes etched in white. Lying just beyond the "best evolved barrier islands in the world" in the photograph, dark water bodies form the greatest collection of brackish-water sounds in America: Currituck, Albemarle, Pamlico, Ocracoke, Roanoke, Core, Bogue and Croatan. Roanoke Island, the cradle of English America, is just visible. Here the first attempted permanent English colony in the New World appeared in 1587 and quickly vanished. Only the Outer Banks, with their snow-white dunes, know the answer to the riddle of the Lost Colony, and their only voice is the boom of distant waves and the endless rattle of sea oats moving with the wind.

When Philip Amadas and Arthur Barlow, dispatched by Sir Walter Raleigh to find a suitable site for a colony, sailed into North Carolina's waters in 1584, they "smealt so sweet and so strong a smell, as if we had ben amid some delicate garden abounding with all kinds of odiferous flowers." They returned to England to describe it to Sir Walter Raleigh and Queen Elizabeth. Other questing visionaries already had left their footprints in North Carolina's soil during the dawn of the "discovery" of the New World. Hernando de Soto and his men, dressed in armor, clanked across North Carolina's primeval wilderness in the year 1540. In search of gold, they had no interest in the flora and fauna of this forbidding place that, because of its geography, claimed a unique place in American history.

From its Outer Banks to its Blue Ridge Mountains, the "Goodliest Land" offered both a blessing and a curse to all who came. From outer space, the barrier islands seem strikingly beautiful and intriguing, yet to the sea captain in the age of sail, they were damning impediments. Had North Carolina possessed a coastline like Virginia, with a Chesapeake Bay and James River, it might have spawned a Richmond of its own. Or, with an Ashley-Cooper River mouth and a safe harbor, North Carolina might have had a Charleston of its own. But the state had neither, only the unrelenting "Graveyard of the Atlantic," 300 miles of barrier islands sealing off the coastline. North Carolinians eventually hailed them as a gem in their state's crown, but during the colonial era pirates lurked in the waters of Ocracoke Sound, plundering vessels that traded between the young colonies and the West Indies. Civil War blockade runners brought arms, food and manufactured goods through the Outer Banks to sustain the Confederate army. The environmentally unique dunes, with their eternal winds, attracted two bicycle mechanics named Orville and Wilbur Wright from Ohio who, in the year 1903, made the first powered flight in history. The tidal estuaries created by the Outer Banks, second in size only to Chesapeake Bay on the east coast, provide a valuable habitat for fish and wildlife. Wild ponies roam Shackleford Banks, descendants of hardy survivors that swam ashore from foundered ships. Bass fishermen and waterfowl hunters make the area world-famous. The Pea Island Refuge, now an important stopover for snow geese, black brant, terns and other avian world travelers, attracts bird watchers from all over the U.S.

West of the Outer Banks, the Coastal Plains—once the bed of an ancient sea—held its own mixed blessings for early Europeans. Once ruled by a powerful and war-like Indian nation, the Tuscaroras, it became a vast area of rich farmland, supporting large plantations dependent on slave labor. In addition to the rich agriculture that characterized the region, vast stands of pine fostered the naval-stores industry, one of North Carolina's principal sources of income during colonial days. Exports of rosin, turpentine, pitch and tar supported ship-builders worldwide.

GLENN VAN NIMWEGEN

7

Valley fog at Mile 348 of the Blue Ridge Parkway, Mitchell.

ling was bent, so grew the tree. North Carolina became the crucible from which some of the first demands for independence issued.

The Piedmont had its own peculiar mix of blessings and curses. The area was settled primarily by Scotch-Irish and Germans who came down the Great Wagon Road from Philadelphia through the Shenandoah Valley of Virginia, into the Yadkin River Country of North Carolina. These hardy frontiersmen favored free labor, harbored democratic ideals and farmed small tracts of the less-fertile soil of the rolling Piedmont. They had little in common with the planter-aristocrats to the east. To make the growing sectionalism within the state worse, all the major rivers of the Piedmont drained southeast into South Carolina, channeling commerce out of the state and promoting independence rather than ties between North Carolina trade centers.

The rolling Piedmont's swift rivers, perfect power for sawmills and millstones, quickly developed into the manufacturing region of the young colony. On November 17, 1753, 15 unmarried men of German descent arrived from Bethlehem, in the Pennsylvania colony. They named their settlement Wachovia, from the German "Wach" and "Ave," meaning "meadow stream." By the end of the next year, the village possessed a carpentry shop, flour mill, pottery, tannery, smithy and shoe shop. By 1786, every house in the nearby hamlet of Salem used water piped in by "conduits." The industry of the Germans found its perfect environment in North Carolina's Piedmont.

The Scotch-Irish, no less industrious than their German brethren, flowed into the Piedmont region via the Great Wagon Road, or "the Bad Road" as it was known among those who traveled it. By the tens of thousands they came, spilling from the Shenandoah Valley of Virginia into North Carolina's Piedmont and mountain regions. Since they were not Irish at all, but were Lowland Scots invited into northern Ireland in 1600s by King James I of England, they took umbrage in being called "Irish." Their thrift and stubbornness were proverbial. A Scotch-Irish prayer of the North Carolina back country asked: "Lord, grant that I may always be right, for Thou knowest that I am hard to turn."

While the Tidewater and Coastal Plain suited agriculture perfectly and changed little to the present day, the Piedmont's swift rivers, lumber and other natural assets invited industry and people to set it in motion. Salem became the first community in the state with electric power in 1898, thanks to the state's first dam on the Yadkin River. Forests provided the cabinet wood that made the High Point Furniture Company, founded in 1888, the

The Tidewater region became a great producer of tobacco, beans, corn, pork and potatoes. Exclusively English stock settled this area, spilling south from the colony at Jamestown, Virginia. Two cultures evolved here, one based on a landed-gentry class modeled after England's, dependent on slave labor, and the other consisting of dirt-poor small farmers and freed indentured servants.

However, here, too, the Devil had his due. The Coastal Plain, cut off from the sea, could not export directly. The eight Lords Proprietors soon deemed it "unprofitable" and neglected it. Yet the early Tar Heels thrived on this neglect and enjoyed the first real independence of the colonies. In the direction the sap-

The Piedmont's industrialization during Reconstruction attracted rural families into growing cities.

first such concern in the state, manufacturing wooden beds and sideboards. By the year 1900, 44 furniture factories operated in High Point alone.

While furniture factories employed primarily men to operate the lathes and saws, the work force that operated the looms of North Carolina's textile industry consisted principally of women and children. By 1900, 90 percent of the state's cotton mills were located in the Piedmont. At about this time the textile industry, previously based on local enterprise, began to attract northern capital. In 1895, Ceasar and Moses Cone moved south from Baltimore to open textile mills in Greensboro. By 1951, North Carolina boasted 939 textile mills and led the nation in producing cotton goods and nylon hosiery.

Tobacco, whose cultivation the colonists adopted from the Indians, quickly became the real money-maker for the young colony and never relinquished that position. Workers rolled the round 1,000-pound hogsheads by the thousands onto sailing vessels bound for England. At the close of the Civil War young James Buchannan "Buck" Duke began to peddle tobacco from a wagon to soldiers wearing both blue and gray. The first tobacco factory, built in Winston in 1871, manufactured 20,000 pounds of chewing tobacco that year. Within 30 years Duke dominated in the cigarette market in the United States with his American Tobacco Company. He became a multi-millionaire and headed one of America's most powerful trusts. By 1945, Tar Heels were saying that the North Carolina tobacco crop was worth more than "all the wheat in Kansas, or all the pigs in Iowa, or all the cotton in Mississippi." By the approach of War World II most production occurred in the northern Piedmont, central Coastal Plains, South Carolina border counties in the Coastal Plain and Burley Belt in the mountains.

The industrialization of the Piedmont during Reconstruction ushered in a new era of optimism and profoundly affected North Carolina life. People left the rural regions of the state and moved to the cities, creating centers of wealth, energy and culture. From 1870 to 1900 the number of towns exceeding 10,000 inhabitants increased from one (Wilmington) to 10 (including Wilmington, Charlotte, Asheville, Winston-Salem, Raleigh and Greensboro).

Tobacco farming has changed but little since this turn-of-the-century view, with workers still suckering, pulling and picking the broad green leaves in summertime.

9

Terns and gulls on Cape Hatteras National Seashore.

Higher education benefitted from the fortunes made in North Carolina's industries. In 1924, "Buck" Duke created the Duke Endowment of about $40 million to aid educational institutions, orphanages and hospitals. Upon his death in 1925, the endowment doubled to more than $80 million, the South's largest endowment ever. Much of it profited Trinity College in Durham, which changed its name to Duke University and became one of the nation's most prestigious private universities.

If dynamism and progress characterize the Piedmont in this state of extremes, then traditions characterize North Carolina's mountain regions. People here cling tenaciously to the old ways. Extraordinarily rich in folklore and crafts, they live among mountains even more resistant to change. In this region where every misty blue mountain ridge recedes into another, we find the highest peaks and most dramatic topography of the entire Appalachian chain. Within North Carolina borders, more than 40 peaks rise above 6,000 feet and 80 peaks stand between 5,000 and 6,000 feet. Here the Blue Ridge Parkway and the Appalachian Trail wind through what the *Encyclopædia Britannica* calls "one of the great floral provinces…the best and most extensive broad-leaf deciduous forests on earth."

The coves and glades sheltered settlers who were independent, brave and earthy. They found the mighty Cherokee Nation living handsomely in the region. The Indians lived in villages of log huts and cultivated maize, beans, sweet potatoes, squash and fruits. William Bartram, a botanist, said of them, "As moral men they certainly stand in no need of European civilization." Inevitably, that mighty Cherokee Nation, one of the two largest and most warlike tribes on the North American continent, clashed with the equally proud Scotch-Irish and English settlers, and blood was spilled. An Indian agent in the late 1700s said, "Every spring, every ford, every path, every farm, every trail, every house, nearly, in its settlement, was once the scene of danger, exposure, attack, exploit, achievement, and death."

The hills reminded the Scotch-Irish of the Scottish Highlands. They invited their brethren from the Pennsylvania colony. They populated the region until they were "thick as fiddlers in hell," to use a mountain expression, and brought with them their superstitions. If a young girl let the teapot boil dry, she would lose her sweetheart. If she cut her hand while peeling onions, she would not marry. If a picture fell from the wall, there would be a death in the family.

One of the most fascinating and least-known facets of the American Revolution is the role played by the mountain men of this region. The early days of the war for independence did not go well for Washington's Continental Army. Except for one victory at Saratoga, New York, the war punished the rebellious colonists. The winters of 1777 at Valley Forge and 1779 at Morristown, New Jersey were abyssmal. Then Charleston fell in May of 1780. The British captured seven American generals, 290 officers, and 5,000 men. Then the Americans suffered the crushing defeat in August 1780 at Camden, South Carolina, where General Gates with 3,052 men was routed by a British force of only 2,000. The patriots lost 800 killed and 1,000 captured. In 1781, half-naked, ill-paid troops of the Pennsylvania line mutinied, demanding discharges for those who had enlisted only for three years.

The American Revolution faltered. Militias stacked their arms and headed home, considering the rebellion finished. Then the eloquent British Major Patrick Ferguson, a Scot himself, raided the North Carolina mountains and tried to muster new conscripts for the British army. He vowed he would hang all the men who opposed him, and burn their farms.

The mountain men rendezvoused at Sycamore Shoals on the Watauga River on September 25, 1781 in what was still part of the North Carolina colony. They vowed to "git" Major Ferguson. From 1,800 men, they selected 900 mounted riflemen—each

armed with a knife, a pouch of parched corn, a power horn, a shot bag and a deadly Pennsylvania rifle—to bring the arrogant Ferguson to bay. This armed force dressed in buckskins created itself out of sheer hatred for the British, not in association with Washington's Continental Army or any state militia. Expert woodsmen all, they knew tricks that served them well when they faced the British. To remedy the problem of "misfires" during rainy weather, for example, they carried small leather "hoods" made of the elbow skin of cows' forelegs, to cover the flintlocks of their rifles.

A survivor from the British force later described the mountain men as "seeming like devils from the infernal regions, tall, rawboned, sinewy, with long matted hair." They marched practically non-stop for approximately 150 miles, penetrating South Carolina by three miles. As they closed in on Ferguson's force, they marched through the entire night of October 6, in rain, to reach the base of Kings Mountain. They attacked without pausing to eat or rest, utterly destroying Ferguson's force of 900 men, killing Ferguson himself.

"Seeming like devils from the infernal regions," mountain men from North Carolina achieved a major Revolutionary War victory.

Left: *Hang gliding on Jockey's Ridge, the Outer Banks.*
Above: *Shore-based menhaden fishery, Carteret County, circa 1910.*

11

The Fate of the Lost Colony

In the year 1587, Governor John White arrived on Roanoke Island with 110 settlers, including 17 women and nine children, in the first attempt at a permanent English settlement in the New World. The colonists had been instructed to locate in the Chesapeake Bay region of Virginia, but when they stopped for remnants of an all-male colony planted on Roanoke Island several years earlier, Captain Fernandez abandoned them. They found no trace of the 18 men they sought, foreshadowing their own fate. Having no choice but to make the best of their situation, they began building structures and preparing the fields for planting. The colony enjoyed good success initially and spirits ran high when the men and women of the settlement petitioned John White to return to England for more supplies. The first child born of English parents in the New World, Virginia Dare, was born here on August 18, 1587.

The colonists agreed that, if they were forced to move, they would carve the name of the new location on a conspicuous tree. If they were endangered, pre-sumably by Indians, they would carve a cross above the word they left on the tree.

John White returned to England to find the nation preparing for war with the invincible Spanish Armada. No one had time or patience to listen to his pleas for his colony. Not until March of 1590, three years later, was he able to return. White anchored off Hatteras and rowed into the sheltered waters of Roanoke Sound in a long boat, where he expected to find his colony. There he found the words "Croatoan" and "Cro," both names referring to a nearby village of the Hatteras Indians. There was no cross carved over the words. That evening White returned to the ship riding the deep waters off Cape Hatteras. He planned to sail to the village of Croatoan the next morning, confident his colonists were in good health. But a vicious storm during the night broke anchor lines and threatened to blow the ship onto the treacherous shoals of the Outer Banks. Low on provisions after the Atlantic crossing, the crew had no choice but to steer toward the West Indies in the darkness, as the storm lashed the canvas of their sails. They planned to return to the Roanoke Colony the next spring, but they encountered more problems in the Indies, which forced them to return to England. In the meantime, Sir Walter Raleigh, who had financed the Roanoke colony, had fallen from grace. A new monarch, James I, who feared Raleigh, ascended the throne, placed Raleigh in the Tower of London, and finally beheaded him. No other ship ventured to check on the first permanent English colony in America until 1602, and no one ever heard from the colonists again.

The explorer and chronicler John Lederer mentioned that, when he travelled the region 70 years later, the Indians of the area had beards and gray eyes. Settlers drifting south from the successful Jamestown, Virginia colony in 1715, more than 100 years later, reported that they found the descendants of the Hatteras tribe tilling soil, holding Indian slaves and speaking English. Some of the names of the original colonists were still in use. About the same time, John Lawson, in his journal, *A New Voyage to Carolina*, wrote that some Hatteras Indians told him their ancestors had been white people.

Various theories attempt to explain the fate of the Lost Colony. The colonists might have tried to sail one of John White's ships back to England and perished at sea. Based on records of early missionaries, the "Lost Colonists" might have been taken in by the Hatteras tribe, only to be killed or enslaved with their hosts by other, more-powerful Indian tribes. Or, Spaniards of the St. Augustine, Florida colony might have destroyed the Roanoke Island settlement, seeing it as a threat to Spanish domination of the New World.

The Elizabeth II, replica
*of a 16-century sailing
vessel like the ones that
brought England's first
colonists.*

CHIP HENDERSON

13

The Early Inhabitants

Above: *A John White drawing of Indian life.*

Facing page: *De Bry engraving of the Indian village "Secota."*

John Lawson, one of the first Englishmen to study and record the Indian tribes of the North Carolina region, heard of the Carolina region from a gentleman he met on the way to Rome in the late 1600s. He was told that the Carolina colony was a bountiful land, where a young man might find adventure. He arrived in 1700 in Charleston, since North Carolina had no seaport. He proceeded to North Carolina on foot, traveling 1,000 miles and compiling his journal, *A New Voyage to Carolina*. However, before leaving Charleston he learned of an event that presaged the fate of the North American Indians confronted by Europeans.

The Sewee tribe had begun to trade with settlers, and grew fond of the goods they offered. They observed that all the ships bringing the iron pots, mirrors and guns they coveted came into view from a certain direction. The Sewee decided that in precisely that direction lay the source of what they wanted. They reasoned that they could profit hugely by eliminating the "middlemen," the traders, by taking their furs and skins directly to the land of the white people. So they constructed huge canoes and fitted them with sails. Finally, most of the men of the tiny Sewee nation left, bound for doom or glory. They could not comprehend that England lay across a vast ocean. They all perished.

Before the coming of the white man only 35,000 Indians inhabited all of North Carolina. John Lawson wrote of them, "They are really better to us than we have been to them, as they always really give us of their victuals at their quarters, while we let them walk by our doors hungry…We look upon them with distain and scorn and think of them as beasts in human form."

John White, governor of the failed Roanoke Island colony, noted that the Indians usually lived in round, not conical, tents made of animal skins tied or woven together. Some tribes built huts or houses. Cooking was primitive: meat on sharp sticks broiled over fire, and other foods roasted directly in hot ashes. Women did the planting, cultivating and harvesting. Most tribes held women in high esteem and practiced monogamy. However, the Tuscaroras were noted for their "trade women."

The Indians, very religious, believed in a Great Spirit and an afterlife. They found it hard to reconcile Christian teachings with the settlers' actions.

Many small tribes inhabited the coastal Carolina region, but even the earliest Europeans found that most had dwindled to mere remnants, sometimes mustering fewer than two dozen warriors. The Indians, having occupied the coastal region only for about 1,000 years themselves, had been decimated by warfare among themselves, and the arrival of the first Europeans brought smallpox. Few of these tribes offered any resistance to the settlers.

The Tuscaroras, though, were by far the most powerful Indian nation in eastern North Carolina. At one time they mustered an estimated 6,000 warriors, but this fighting force had dwindled to only 1,200 when the Europeans arrived. John Lederer described a haughty Tuscarora chief as "the most proud, imperious barbarian" he met in all his travels. For 50 years they lived in peace with the whites as the smaller tribes of the coastal plain— the Hatteras, Chowanocs, Nottaways and Pamlicos—disappeared beneath the tide of colonists. But the Tuscaroras, enraged by their mistreatment at the hands of whites, attacked the settlement of New Bern on September 22, 1711, killing more than 200 men, women and children, nearly wiping out the entire population of the region. Troops from South Carolina arrived to help the colonists win the Tuscarora War.

Little remains of the coastal Indian tribes who greeted the first Europeans on the beaches of the Outer Banks with offerings of fish and taught them about native crops, except for a few Indian place names such Currituck, Pasquotank, Perquimans, Croatan, Manteo and Wanchese.

The most powerful tribe of the Piedmont section, the Catawbas, dwelt between the Catawba and Yadkin rivers and numbered about 7,000. They faced determined enemies to the east and west of them in the Tuscarora and Cherokee nations, respectively. They eagerly allied themselves, therefore, with the colonists in the Tuscarora War and again joined them to fight the Cherokees and the British in the American Revolution. In 1738 and 1758, epidemics of smallpox thinned the tribe by one half. South Carolina, remembering the Catawba warriors who helped it fight the British, took steps to save the nation, giving the tribe lands in what are now York and Lancaster counties. However, the Catawbas were a nation in ruin. By 1784 they numbered 250 and by 1826 only 110.

The Cherokee nation never accepted the yoke of the white man. Of Iroquoian stock, the Cherokees come to the Carolina highlands after they were driven out of the headwaters region of the Ohio River long before Europeans came to the New World. Their new territory covered the entire region from upper Georgia to the Ohio River, including the rich hunting grounds of Kentucky. The Cherokees displaced the Shawnees, the original claimants. In 1735, the Cherokee tribe numbered about 17,000 but they, too, endured a smallpox epidemic in 1738.

The Royal Proclamation of 1763 protected Cherokee lands from land-grabbing colonists, but nothing could stop the immigrants who slipped into the vast forests claimed by the Cherokees. In 1776, seeing no hope of stopping the invasion by lawless settlers, the Cherokees allied themselves with the British during the American Revolution. In retribution, 6,000 Georgians and Carolinians destroyed Cherokee towns and killed all who could not escape, selling the surviving children into slavery. Some Cherokees fled into the mountains, where they lived on the brink of starvation for years. Still, they managed to weather the American Revolution with 43,000 square miles of declared territory, which the whites coveted. The final humiliation of the Cherokee Nation came in 1824, with the discovery of gold in north Georgia and the election of Indian-hating Andrew Jackson as President.

All the efforts of the Cherokees to adapt to the whites, from governing themselves through an elected legislature, to adopting the U.S. Constitution, to accepting vastly diminished borders, were forgotten with the discovery of gold in Cabarrus County, in 1801, and the influx of prospectors. Georgia declared their legal rights abrogated and appropriated all their lands within the state.

NORTH CAROLINA DIV. OF ARCHIVES & HISTORY IMAGES BOTH PAGES

General Winfield Scott captured 14,000 Cherokees and marched them out of their beloved, verdant mountains to dusty Oklahoma on the "Trail of Tears" in 1838, following President Jackson's orders. One quarter of them would die. Still, approximately 1,000 of the proudest Cherokees escaped once again by hiding in the remotest places where the Appalachian Trail now winds. During this critical time, white families befriended many of the Cherokees in hiding. Those who barely survived on roots and berries heard the ring of axes in every cove and glade. Their descendants watched the hardwood forest cut by loggers and hauled away by locomotives.

During the American colonial era, Indians in the Carolina region and elsewhere favored the French in the ongoing "duel of the traders" between Britain and France. The tribes showed great respect for the French traders, who opened the way for fur trappers, hunters and, later, settlers. Wherever the English went, they introduced the concepts of a class society and segregated themselves from the natives. The French, however, embraced the hedonism of hunter-gathers wherever they found it, from North America to Tahiti to Vietnam. William Byrd in his famous *History of the Dividing Line* observed in 18th-century America:

"The French, for their Parts have not been so Squeamish in Canada, who upon trial find abundance of attraction in the Indians. Their late Grand Monarch thought it not below even the dignity of a Frenchman to become one flesh with this People, and therefore Ordered 100 Livres for any of his Subjects, Man or Woman that will intermarry with a Native.

"By this piece of policy we find the French Interest very much strengthened amongst the Savages, and their Religion, such as it is, propagated just as far as their Love. And I heartily wish the well-concerted scheme don't hereafter give the French an Advantage over his Majesty's good Subjects on the Northern Continent of America."

John Lawson, in his *A New Voyage*, noted that the English traders brought lavish appointments into the wilderness while the French lived simply, no better than or differently from the Indians themselves:

"The French being a temperate industrious People, some of them bringing very little Effects, yet by their Endeavors and mutual Assistance amongst themselves, have out-stripped our English, who brought with'em larger Fortunes, thou less endeavor to manage their Talents to the best Advantage."

The earliest European settlers in the North Carolina colony were the English who trickled south from their first successful colony in the New World, Jamestown, Virginia, established in

Banished to dusty Oklahoma on the "Trail of Tears" in 1838, about 1,000 Cherokees escaped into the Appalachians and stayed here.

1607 just north of the failed Roanoke Island colony. In the 20 years following Jamestown's settlement, 10,000 colonists entered the waters of Chesapeake Bay, yet not a ship landed along the North Carolina coast for want of a seaport. The new arrivals in the Carolina colony found that, for the first time in their experience, small farmers or former indentured servants could obtain land and ascend the social ladder. Here, the social classes tended to mix. By hard work, strategic marriages or lucky land deals, many small farmers and artisans became gentlefolk. Many of North Carolina's planters were self-made men.

Society consisted basically of four classes, headed by gentry or planter aristocracy, which constituted only five percent of the population. Below this ranked in order farmers, indentured or "Christian" servants, and slaves. In Virginia, the class divisions were more rigid because of the stronger ties to England. The English, seeking to preserve their social system in the New World, enacted the "Fundamental Constitutions"—designed to "avoid a numerous democracy"—that classified society into strata ranging from degrees of nobility down to the lowest social class of "leet" men and provided that "all children of leet men" should remain leet men "to all generations."

Many individuals who could not pay their way to the New World signed contracts, usually for two to five years, as indentured servants. "Indents" included felons, paupers, political prisoners, and those swindled by unscrupulous ship captains. They came primarily from England and Ireland. Those who fulfilled the terms of contract were granted freedom and 50 acres of land. They were proud of their new titles such as "farmer," "yeoman," or "husbandman." The indentured servant concept was, in general, a positive factor for the young colony.

Left: *Threshing rye in the North Carolina mountains using a "hit or miss" engine, 1912.*

Facing page: *Before electricity reached the mountains, family laundry required a whole day.*

17

North Carolinians suffered through an ongoing dispute with Virginia over the location of the colonies' mutual border. North Carolina hoped that a careful survey would show that the mouth of the Nansemond River was in North Carolina, thus giving it a port from which to ship tobacco. But North Carolina never would have an open port during the colonial era, and Virginia taxed North Carolina tobacco heavily when it was shipped from Norfolk. In order to gain a further monopoly, Virginia refused to export North Carolina tobacco altogether from 1679 until 1731.

A final bone of contention between the Royal Colony of Virginia—with strong ties with England—and North Carolina—a "proprietary" or second-generation colony—was the ongoing rumor that Virginia might claim the Albemarle region of North Carolina as part of Virginia. Virginians considered the region was seen as a place settled by "idle debtors," "theaves," "pyrates" and "run-away servants."

The colonists lived mainly by subsistence farming and bought only salt and iron goods. Hogs and cattle were minor cash crops. Cloth was made at home—in every log house were spinning wheel and loom to convert flax and wool into cloth—as were soap and candles. The colonists added Indian crops to their own, the principal ones being corn, wheat and rice, and tobacco, the leading money crop. Tobacco cultivation then was much the same as today, involving seed beds, transplanting, worming, priming and suckering.

Lumber was an important trade item for the young Carolina colony, which exported 30 million board feet of lumber in 1764. One seventh of all lumber products from the new colonies came from North Carolina. As all commodities were shipped in casks, barrels and hogsheads, cooperage was one of the largest industries.

The earliest reference to black slaves in the colony was in 1694, when five individuals claimed rights to extra land for having brought in eight black slaves. As early as 1665, the Lords Proprietors in England offered all "masters" 80 acres of land for each male indentured servant, and 50 acres for each slave. With this incentive, the number of slaves in the eastern counties grew swiftly. By 1790, the slave population was above 100,000, one third of the state's total population.

Slaves sometimes accumulated enough money to buy their freedom, and children took the status of their mothers. Hundreds of planters freed their slaves in their wills. By 1860, 30,463 North Carolina slaves were freed out of a total 311,059. The Quakers and Moravians organized societies dedicated to emancipation. By 1825, the Quakers' North Carolina Manumission Society claimed 28 local chapters and more than 1,000 members. The American

Abundant game resources, self-sufficiency and subsistence farming supported the colonists.

Colonization Society also was active in the state and took credit for the emancipation of about 2,000 slaves in a three-year period.

While North Carolina's settlement began in the 1600s with primarily English stock, in the 1700s some Germans, additional English, and a great many Scotch-Irish immigrants arrived in the New World. Many German people were driven from their homes by French invaders, misruled by their own monarchs, and ruined by the terrible winter of 1708-1709. Beginning in central Pennsylvania, German immigrants constructed great barns and dotted the valleys with neat, plowed fields. By 1760, they had reached the New River country of North Carolina and Virginia and had converted the trackless wilderness from the Pennsylvania colony southward into productive agricultural land.

It was rich land for hunters as well as farmers. In his diary, Dr. Thomas Walker, who surveyed land in the Shenandoah Valley region in the year 1749 for the Loyal Land Company, tallied: "We killed in the journey thirteen buffaloes, eight elks, fifty-three bears, twenty deer, four wild geese and about 150 turkeys, beside small game. We might have killed three times as much meat if we had wanted it."

One of the Germans' greatest contributions was in education, for the colonial government did practically nothing in this regard. There were no free public schools; most of the early efforts towards education were undertaken by the church. In the early German and Scotch-Irish settlements, a church and a school house sprang up at the same time as the community itself. In 1767, near the present city of Greensboro, the Reverend David Caldwell founded his famous "Log College," enrolling 50 to 60 students each year. This institution was a "classical school" serving as an "academy, a college and a theological seminary" and was then the most important educational institution in North Carolina.

The German schools were taught by German-speaking instructors. These people did not blend with the other colonists, but tended to segregate themselves in order to keep their religious, social and economic customs intact. Never having never been exposed to slavery in the Old World, the German colonist relied on his own labor. He became the best farmer in the region.

But the great majority of settlers were the Scotch-Irish and English. They filled the valleys, from the Piedmont to the remotest areas of the Cherokees' ancestral hunting grounds in western North Carolina and what would become the state of Tennessee (in 1796). In the year of 1765, 1,000 wagons rolled through Salisbury, North Carolina, bound for the vacant lands

Left: *Working with oxen in western North Carolina.*

Facing page: *Spinning yarn, weaving cloth and sewing clothing were part of self-sufficient living from North Carolina's colonial days.*

19

Above: In the 19th century, visitors often vacationed in wagons and carriages to learn more about land available in North Carolina.

Facing page: Once an unruly colony and then an independent-minded state, North Carolina gained much of its Tar Heel toughness from its heritage of mountain inaccessibilty and outer banks remoteness.

to the west. The *South Carolina and American General Gazette* commented three years later, "There was scarce any history, either ancient or modern which affords an account of such a rapid and sudden increase of inhabitants in a backfrontier country as that of North Carolina."

William Bartram, the leading botanist of the colonial era, who explored the remotest and most dangerous areas of the colonies, chronicling every plant, flower, tree and shrub, was born in 1739. At that time, settlement of the wild, mountainous regions had progressed only to the Shenandoah Valley of Virginia. The Cherokee nation still ruled the Blue Ridge. Yet, when Bartram died in 1823, wealthy Charlestonians were traveling by carriage to summer homes near Flat Rock, south of Asheville. Such was the strength and swiftness of the tide of settlers searching for their own land.

Because of the isolation caused by North Carolina's Outer Banks, the colony had probably the most unsatisfactory relationship with the Crown, among the 13 original colonies. It led to many historic political firsts within the borders of "the Colony Different." Culpepper's Rebellion of 1677 was the first popular uprising in any of the colonies, and was caused by intolerable British mercantile policies that stated all colonial

goods must be shipped on British ships and that all North Carolina tobacco must go to England.

The Watauga Association in 1772 created one of the first free and independent governments, democratic in spirit and representative in form, conceived on the American continent. Independent back-country settlers, far from the North Carolina colonial capital in New Bern, assembled at Sycamore Shoals, near present Elizabethtown, Tennessee, negotiated their own lands from the Cherokees and created their own independent territory: "The Washington District of North Carolina."

In Brunswick in the year 1765, soon after the British Parliament passed the Stamp Act, which proclaimed that all documents, newspapers and bills of lading must bear stamps proving that high document taxes had been paid, the North Carolina colonists lodged their protest. In one of the first acts of armed resistance to the authority of the English Crown, angry colonists surrounded the residence of Royal Governor William Tryon and placed him under house arrest. Stamps never were used on the mercantile traffic of the Cape Fear River. North Carolina's resistance to the Stamp Act was the most effective of any American colony's.

The Halifax Resolves, penned on April 12, 1776 at the Roanoke River port, was the first official state action in which a colony demanded its independence. It furthermore recommended to the Continental Congress that *all* the colonies should declare their independence from the British crown.

But the most famous and most controversial of all North Carolina firsts was the "Mecklenburg Declaration of Independence of May 20, 1775." The original document never has been found, and countless books and articles have supported and denounced its existence. However, the date May 20, 1775 appears on the North Carolina flag in honor of the Mecklenburg Declaration. Both British commander Charles Cornwallis and General Tarleton referred to the village of Charlotte as "the most hostile to England of any in America" and Mecklenburgers are proud this day that their forebears were the first in all the colonies to declare themselves free and independent people.

In 1788, the North Carolina Constitutional Convention, held at Hillsborough, refused to ratify the United States Constitution since it had no Bill of Rights. True to form, "the Colony Different" showed intense distrust of distant powerful governing bodies and insisted passionately on protection of personal freedoms.

FACING PAGE: JOHN RUCKER

The Land: From Barrier Islands To Southern Highlands

Above: Ocracoke Island tranquility.

Facing page: Sunset on Pamlico Sound at Goose Creek State Park.

N orth Carolina's geological history is extremely complex; probably no other state has seen greater geological transformation. The state's three primary divisions today each differ drastically from their pasts.

The Atlantic Ocean has risen and fallen. At the close of the Mesozoic Era, the Age of Dinosaurs, the coastline began approximately where the cities of Rocky Mount, Raleigh and Rockingham now stand. Yet the Wisconsin glacial advance 10,000 years ago locked much of the earth's water in glacial ice, lowered the Atlantic 300 feet, and pushed the shoreline of North Carolina perhaps 50 miles farther east than at present.

Where the Blue Ridge Mountains now stand, stretching from the North Carolina foothills to the Tennessee border, a vast arm of the sea once ebbed and surged. To the east of this gulf, where the Piedmont now sprawls, a great spine of mountains called the Ocoee Range stretched from the Northern Gulf of Mexico to Virginia. The Ocoees rose as high as the modern Swiss Alps, and scientists call the entire region Old Appalachia. Since no forests evolved to protect the slopes of the Ocoees from erosion, they rapidly wore down to the gently sloping hills of North Carolina's Piedmont, with elevations of only 350 to 1800 feet. The highest elevations of the Piedmont area mark the few erosion-resistant remnants of the Ocoees, known as *monadnocks*. These include the Uwharries of Montgomery and Randolph counties, the Sauratown Mountains of Stokes and Surry counties, the Kings Mountain Range of Cleveland and Gaston counties, the Brushy Mountains of Wilkes County and the South Mountains in Burke and Rutherford counties. Hanging Rock and Pilot Mountain are also included in this group.

At the end of the Paleozoic Era, earth's tumultuous crust thrust what we now know as the Appalachian Chain up from the bed of the ancient sea that once lapped at the feet of the Ocoees. Sedimentary rocks created by accumulations on the floor of the sea combined with older "basement complex" rocks to create complex thrust belts and fault lines that formed mountains possibly greater than any on earth today. These were the Appa-lachians before 270 million years of erosion transformed them from peaks taller than the Rockies to the gentle, rounded, topsoil-covered Smokies.

Driving through the gentle hills west of Winston-Salem, it is hard to imagine that the snow-capped Ocoees once stood here, as mighty as the Swiss Alps of today. In the clouds along the Blue Ridge Parkway, it is even harder to imagine that the Blue Ridge region once formed the bed of an ancient sea, which was buckled, folded and upthrust into massive peaks, only to be weathered into the loamy-soiled Blue Ridge and Smoky Mountain ranges.

The Atlantic Ocean is invading the mainland once again. Water bodies such as Pamlico and Albemarle sounds, simply flooded river valleys, once stood well inland during the last glacial age. The Atlantic invaded North Carolina six times in the geological past and left a "terrace" each time. These terraces appear today in the Coastal Plain, which stretches from the coastline inland for nearly 150 miles, rising about one foot per mile.

The Outer Banks, which form the leading edge of North Carolina's coastline, probably resulted when breaker and undertow action caused sedimentary material to form reefs parallel to the shore line. They vary in width from two miles to only a few hundred yards and are characterized by hummocks of sand and many large dunes, some higher than a hundred feet. Inlets through the Outer Banks temporarily formed as storm waves surged across these slender barrier islands. Old maps and historical documents record more than two dozen inlets, although only six currently exist, some of them nearly blocked.

Just west of the Outer Banks, the tidewater area begins. This vast, thinly-settled region is generally low-lying, poorly drained and swampy. The wet "low country" or tidewater merges with the black-soiled Coastal Plain gradually, and as the swampy character dissipates into the humus-rich topsoil, a rich farming belt takes its place. The Coastal Plain, generally flat, rises gradually except for the region east of Rockingham known as the Sandhills, which rise to nearly 500 feet.

North Carolina's tidewater region features a group of brackish-

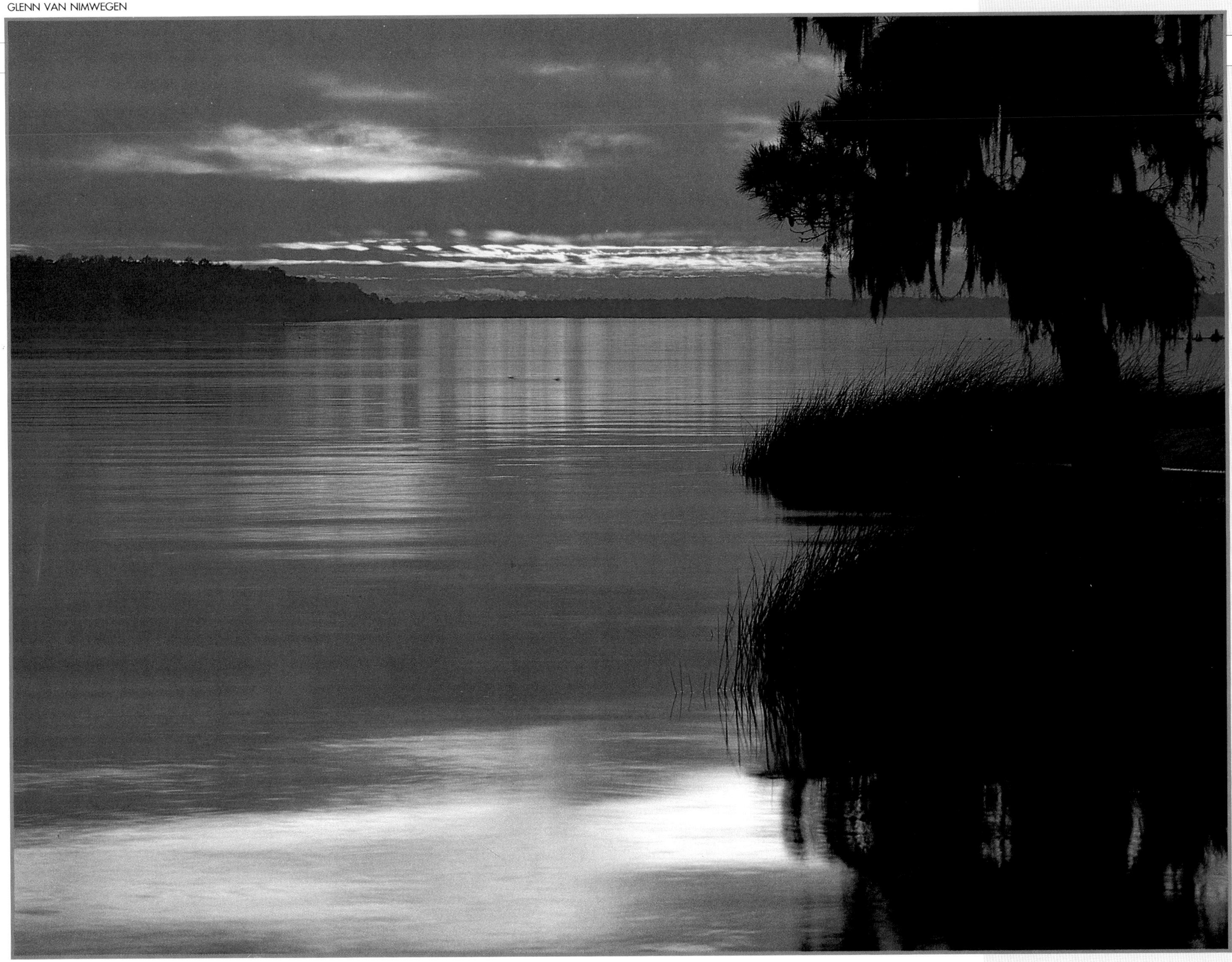

Above: *Tupelo, red maple and Spanish moss at Merchant's Millpond State Park.*

Facing page: *St. James Episcopal Church at Bath is the oldest church in North Carolina.*

Virginia border, the Great Dismal Swamp and other swampy regions cover an area of some 300 square miles. The Great Dismal Swamp probably was a more productive grassland-type ecosystem once. Archaeologists have found numerous *bola* stones in the Dismal Swamp region, indicating that prehistoric man hunted and fished here. The bola, a throwing device consisting of three stones tied to leather thongs, characterized prehistoric man from Alaska to South America. No one knows whether the bola evolved separately in each location, or followed migrating tribes.

Now the Great Dismal Swamp supports swamp-forest flora like swamp gum, cypress and white cedar. William Byrd, who surveyed the swamp in the early 1700s, described it as a "horrible desert" and doubted the area could profit the eight Lords Proprietors.

Another feature of the Tidewater region, the "Carolina Bays," comprises one of the most remarkable and enigmatic physical settings in the world. Scattered across the lower Coastal Plain of North Carolina and South Carolina, an estimated half million shallow, peat-bottomed, dark-colored lakes, all elliptical, lie parallel to each other. The slightly elevated rims of these ponds, which range in size from an acre to several miles in length, consist of coarse white sand. Bay trees line the perimeters of most, and evergreen shrubs cover extensive, level, elevated peat soil areas around them. Indians called these areas *pocosins,* which meant "swamp on a hill." Scientists once thought a meteor shower formed the Carolina Bays, but now believe they formed as receding seas gradually exposed North Carolina's continental shelf. Numerous small ponds remained, eroded on their windward shores by the wave action from unidirectional winds. Lake Waccamaw, in Columbus County, ranks as largest of the Carolina Bay lakes at 5.3 miles long.

In contrast to the dark-watered Carolina Bays, White Lake in Bladen County depends on a huge spring that rises from unknown depths, and is regarded as one of the most beautiful small lakes in the region.

On the broad, flat, ancient sea terraces of the lower Coastal Plain, *scarps*—serpentine scars on the landscape—mark the coastlines of North Carolina during epochs of warm weather. Numerous large lakes, unrelated to the Carolina Bays, include Phelps and Pungo in Washington County, Catfish, Long and Great in Craven County and Alligator and Mattamuskeet in Hyde County. While their dark water discourages development as recreational sites, these large, undisturbed water bodies provide wildlife habitat. Mattamuskeet Wildlife Refuge, the largest, covers 50,000 acres.

The Tidewater region and eastern Coastal Plain support fascinating flora and fauna: Venus's-flytraps, four types of pitcher

water sounds the likes of which no other state can claim. They lie immediately behind the barrier islands, seeming to enjoy their protection from the angry Atlantic. Curricuck Sound is one, a clear, nearly freshwater lagoon made up of numerous islands and freshwater marshes of saw-grass, giant cordgrass and cattails. Largemouth bass attract anglers to this area from all over the nation, although in recent years dry weather has elevated the salinity, temporarily hurting the bass fishing. This area also is exceedingly rich in wildlife. On the mainland side, just beyond sight of the sand ridges of the Outer Banks, with the boom of ocean waves just beyond earshot, the western shorelines of Pamlico and Albemarle sounds present strikingly wild regions where cypress trees grow with flaring "knees" and trunks submerged in up to five feet of water, where Spanish moss hangs from dense swamp forests. This entire estuarine system ranks second in size only to the Chesapeake Bay on the east coast.

The Tidewater Belt runs from 30 to 80 miles inland and supports many other intriguing habitats. To the north, along the plant, wild orchids and irises, red-cockaded woodpeckers, eastern diamondback rattlesnakes and American alligators inhabit Green Swamp, south of Wilmington. Here, The Nature Conservancy, a national conservation group, owns a 15,722-acre preserve. The entire world population of the endangered Colley's Meadowrue is found in the Coastal Plain of North Carolina along the Pender-Onslow county lines, where The Nature Conservancy also maintains the Lanier Quarry Savanna Preserve.

While the Tidewater region's nonporous, peaty soil leaves it poorly drained, swampy and thus lightly populated, the growing towns of Wilmington and Morehead City qualify as North Carolina's only two seaports, capable of accommodating the largest tankers and ocean freighters.

The Coastal Plain is vast, and the Tidewater region is only a small part of it. As one moves west, eastern North Carolina changes little in altitude—yet the loose, dark, fertile soils vastly alter the productivity of the area. On the edge of the southern Tidewater region, the soils foster the state's blueberry industry. High-bush blueberries find the sandy, highly acidic soils much to their liking. Peanut production centers in the northern portion of the middle Coastal Plain benefit from the well drained sandy loam. Peach growers favor the sandhills where the soil and rolling, well drained hills create an ideal environment for this important cash crop.

The Upper Coastal Plain likely will always be the chief agricultural region of the state, for its geology is ideally suited to cultivation. Yet industries seeking to locate in North Carolina are finding this region "untapped" when compared to the Piedmont. The fundamental weakness of this area, its high ratio of tenancy to farm ownership, is a legacy of the earlier cotton and tobacco labor practices.

Each soil user views soil differently, from the highway engineer who wants load-bearing characteristics, to the farmer who wants agricultural productivity, to the real estate developer who wants to know if the soil can percolate waste from septic tanks. Practically all of North Carolina's soils require liberal applications of lime and fertilizer to suit the common root crops and pasture. Acid, infertile soils result from the *leaching*, or loss, of mineral nutrients such as nitrogen, potash and calcium. Long, hot summers and excessive rainfall rob soils of these important ingredients. In the southern portion of North Carolina's mountain region, excessive rainfall already has leached even the relatively young soil deposited as sediment on the bed of the ancient sea. Highlands, in western North Carolina, the wettest place on the East Coast, receives more than 80 inches of rainfall a year.

CHIP HENDERSON

The Piedmont region, with its dynamic economy, blends rural and urban lifestyles.

North Carolina's mild winters provide a pleasant interlude.

The Coastal Plain ends and the hilly Piedmont section begins at the *fall line*, the head of river navigation. Here towns like Roanoke Rapids grew up where water travel terminated because of river rapids. The Piedmont's geology predates that of both the Coastal Plain and the mountains, for the ancient Ocoees predate both the Appalachians and the sea sediments that formed the Coastal Plain. The eroded base of the Ocoee range provided the swift rivers needed to power textile mills and furniture factories as the South recovered from the Civil War. To the present day, Piedmont North Carolina has maintained its regional dynamism. It ranks first in the South in every phase of industrial development.

The Piedmont blends rural and urban. Virtually everyone in this region lives within commuting distance of a non-farm job, yet the area ranks near the top of the United States in numbers of farm people per square mile. Great under-employment of the rural population provides a vast potential labor force, a tremendous asset for industrial development in the next century.

For example, my clogging partner, Novella Hopkins, and her husband, Herbert, live an easy 20-minute drive from Greensboro. Herbert works in a Greensboro chemical factory while Novella manages their little farm, where she maintains a small herd of distinguished-looking goats and breeds basset hounds. She milks the goats daily to classical music and makes yogurt, and fertilizes her large organic garden with goat manure. When I drive into the yard there is always some surprise, a new litter of puppies to see, a gift of delicious goat milk, a new bantam rooster in the chicken pen, a new clogging step to learn. The children all share farm chores and are growing up knowing the unpretentious country ways, yet they enjoy the culture of nearby cities. It is an exceedingly satisfactory arrangement—and an increasingly common one in the Piedmont and, indeed, all across North Carolina.

Despite the heaviest population concentration in the state, more than half the Piedmont still is forest land. Many large man-made reservoirs attract heavy recreational use. Tobacco workers sucker, pull and pick the broad green leaves in summertime. The Piedmont clays provide raw materials for the more than 1 billion bricks that North Carolina produces every year. From North Carolina in 1972 came 15 percent of total U.S. brick production, valued at $47.1 million. The sands, clays and shales of the region also produce sewer pipe, drain tile and cement. Crushed stone and gravel account for more one half of North Carolina's total mineral value annually. The Seagrove area, south of Asheboro, now a world-famous pottery region, has attracted potters since the 1750s with its fine-grained clays. From 1801 until 1849, North Carolina ranked as one of the major gold-producing states

Soil also differs according to the type of parent rock or sediment that forms it. The disintegration of light-colored granitic rocks produces yellowish, acidic soils. The breakdown of dark *basic* or *mafic* rock types produces less-acidic and more-fertile soils, with greater loam content and dark red subsoil. Since the Coastal Plain experienced numerous cycles of invasion during the Ice Age, the sea left sedimentary deposits of varying age, from 20,000 years ago to more than a million years ago. The older soils have experienced greater weathering and leaching and therefore require more fertilizer. Experts have identified more than 200 types of soils in the state, ranging from white sands with little pumice in the sandhills, to the heavy clays of the Piedmont, to the black, high-organic soil of the lower Coastal Plain, to the brown loam of the mountains.

in the Union, giving up one 17-pound nugget in 1799 (it was not assayed for three years) at the Reed Mine in Cabarrus County. Gold and silver still acount for small-scale ventures.

North Carolina's mountain region has earned a reputation for its gemstones. Transylvania and Macon counties contain both sapphires and rubies. Gem fanciers love this area of the state, and Cowee Valley near Murphy draws hundreds to "pan" for precious stones each summer. The Spruce Pine district boasts emeralds.

Since 1917, the state has led the nation in production of feldspar. Extremely high-quality quartz deposits from the Chestnut Flat Mine in Mitchell County provided the raw materials for the Hale telescope at Mt. Palomar, California. Granite generates more capital than any other stone and the area near Mt. Airy contains extremely high-quality stone. The Mt. Airy Granite Quarry is one of the largest and best equipped open-face granite quarries in the world.

The North Carolina mountain region is "apple country." Here the shallow soils combine with good air drainage on the slopes, and cool climate, to create an ideal environment. The North Carolina mountains produced literally hundreds of varieties during the golden age of apples in the late 1800s: L.H. Bailey in his 1922 book mentions that in 1892 nursery catalogs listed more than 800 varieties. Before the automobile opened up the mountains and refrigeration simplified food storage, growers wanted some varieties of apples that "stored" best, others that "cooked" best, or "sliced and dried" best, "tasted" best, "canned" best, and still others that "cidered" best. Today, however, 90 percent of the state's apple crop consists of Red Delicious, Golden Delicious and Rome Beauties.

While apples originated in Persia and were cultivated in Europe for at least 2,000 years before immigrants brought them to the New World, apple trees flourished when introduced to the Southern Highlands. Many almost-forgotten breeds, although facing oblivion, hang on by a stem. Among the little-known strains still grown by specialists are Sheep's Nose, Crow's Egg and yellow Bellflower. Some surviving breeds bear the names of people who developed them: Stark, Betsy Deaton, Black Hoover, Striped Ben Davis and Duckette. Some took names from their distinctive tastes, such as Winesap, Sweet Russell and Spice Apple. The Spitzbergen and the Virginian Beauty were named for their places of origin. Other names are more perplexing, such as Knotley Pea and Democrat. The apple tree was a potent harbinger of spring to the mountain family who watched eagerly for the first buds and blossoms as winter eased its grip on the mountains.

CHIP HENDERSON PHOTOS BOTH PAGES

Trees of many kinds make the mountains this state's most heavily forested area. In many western counties, forests cover as much as 80 percent of the land. Within the mountains, various state, federal and local governments own and administer 1,300,000 acres of forest land.

Two major vegetation systems occur within the North Carolina mountains. Deciduous, or leaf-bearing, trees, generally cover the valleys and slopes up to 5,000 feet, while conifers, or cone-bearing, evergreens generally occur above 5,000 feet. The seasonal changes of the alpine flora make North Carolina's mountain scenery as spectacular as any in the world.

Five major forest types occur in deciduous woodlands on the lower slopes and valleys. Cove hardwood forest of the North Carolina region ranks among the richest, most-complex deciduous forest anywhere on earth. Common tree species include hemlock,

The bounty of mountain-grown apples at a farmers' market.

27

Great Smoky Mountains National Park could be called "Wildflower National Park."

silverbell, yellow buckeye, white basswood, sugar maple, yellow birch, tulip poplar, beech, cucumber tree, fraser magnolia, black cherry, red oak, white oak, white ash, black-gum and chestnut oak. More than 175 tree species grow here, more than in all of Europe. Before Europeans arrived, the North Carolina mountains were covered with the same climax-community forest that stretched to the Tidewater.

One of the major species in the mountains before the 1920s was the chestnut. During the 18th, 19th and early 20th centuries, mountain people as well as deer, bears, wild hogs and other mammals depended on chestnuts when all other protein sources failed. However, in 1903, a fungus parasite from China arrived on nursery stock and by 1920 the resulting "blight" effectively had killed the chestnuts that had, in many areas, made up half the deciduous forest. From their stumps sprout shoots of young trees, but the lingering blight mysteriously kills these before they

reach much more than 15 feet. North Carolinians hope the species will develop a genetic resistance to the blight and regain its eminence in the hardwood forest.

Pioneers looked for the small, flowering dogwood, now the state tree, when they chose their homesteads, for it indicates fertile soil.

Among the most fascinating ecological niches in the forests are the mountain "balds," usually found at the same elevations as spruce-fir forests. "Heath balds" or "laurel slicks" are treeless communities dominated by rhododendrons and mountain laurel. They cover exposed areas of steep terrain above 4,000 feet. Although they appear smooth from a distance (hence the name "slick") they actually form impenetrable thickets (hence the name "laurel hells" used by the local hunters). While laurels may result from burns, they usually represent the climax communities for some sites, in particular on very steep slopes. Grass balds attract hikers eager to enjoy openness that is rare in the mountains. Most grass balds occur above 5,000 feet and support mountain oat grass as well as shrubs such as flame azaleas, blueberries, blackberries and hawthorns.

Approximately 1,500 species of native flowering herbs, shrubs and flowers suggest that Great Smoky Mountains National Park could appropriately be called "Wildflower National Park." Arthur Stupka, Park Naturalist for 25 years, said, "Vegetation is to the Great Smoky Mountains National Park is what granite domes and waterfalls are to Yosemite, geysers are to Yellowstone, and sculptured pinnacles are to Bryce Canyon National Park." Within the park, a few members of subtropical communities survive from preglacial times. Conversely, one also finds northern communities of plant life that migrated southward during the glacial epochs. Near the summits of several peaks are species more commonly found in Canada, including the yellow-flowered Clinton's lily, wood sorrel and witch-hobble.

The best times to enjoy the park's wildflowers are mid-April to mid-May and mid-June through mid-July. From mid-June to mid-July, mountain laurels, rhododendrons, azaleas and heath shrubs put on spectacular displays within access of organized hikes and motor caravans.

The North Carolina mountains harbor intriguing environmental niches unique in the world. The only known population of Schwelnitz groundsel in the Southeast, normally found no farther south than New York's Adirondack Mountains, inhabits the Roan Highlands, near the village of Minneapolis.

The Nature Conservancy's Bluff Mountain preserve is a naturalist's 758-acre dream. Located four miles west of West

North Carolina's climate brings short, mild winters and long, hot, humid summers.

Jefferson, it contains a five-acre *fen* on the top of Bluff Mountain, the only true fen in the southern Appalachians. A fen is a bog that receives its water from nutrient-rich springs rather than runoff. Less acid than a bog, it supports a greater range of species. More than 400 flowering herbs and shrubs have attracted botanists to the Bluff Mountain Preserve ever since Asa Gray's first visit in 1841. The flower show here, unsurpassed in the southern Appalachians, begins in April and continues through October with an ever-changing array of species in bloom.

The brook trout, native to the region, is not a trout at all, but a member of the arctic char family. No one knows how they came to be here. Also within the park, and indeed the entire mountain region, a highly favorable soil substratum makes possible a diverse mushroom population.

Experts designate North Carolina's climate as subtropical, which implies short, mild winters and long, hot, humid summers, with pleasant transitional seasons. Precipitation usually comes as rain during the growing season, but includes several snowfalls each winter. Winter temperatures seldom dip into the single digits for more than a day or two at a time and seldom climb above a hundred degrees for more than a brief spell.

Left: *A Coastal Plain soybean field.*

Facing page: *The Glen Cove Viaduct on the Blue Ridge Parkway.*

Graveyard of the Atlantic

Below: The G.A. Kohler, *a vessel from Baltimore, aground on North Carolina's Outer Banks.*

Facing page: The commercial fishing boat Bailey Boy *wallows in heavy seas off Oregon Inlet.*

Even before the first English colonies sprouted along the East Coast, Spanish sea captains discovered they could save considerable time sailing between the West Indies and Spain by allowing the strong Gulf Stream to carry them northward to Cape Hatteras. They sailed due east as soon as they sighted Cape Hatteras, the correct latitude for an east-west crossing. Cape Hatteras also became the navigational checkpoint for vessels coming from the Old World, bound for points along the east coast. The eyes of many a seafarer, from New England slave traders to blockade runners during the Civil War, strained for that siren spit of sand.

In order to visually locate Hatteras, sailing vessels had to brave some of the most treacherous waters of the known world, the "Graveyard of the Atlantic." The area included most of North Carolina's coastline. Off Cape Hatteras the frigid Virginia Coastal Drift current collided head-on with the warm Gulf Stream current, creating deadly "rips" where waves had no trough or predictable path of travel. Here the waters seemed to leap up in pointed seamounts, as though possessed. The area generated its own weather, creating high winds that whipped the "rip" areas. Underneath the dark waters lay ever-shifting Diamond Shoals, its shallows creating white-crested breakers where startled sea captains expected deep, safe waters. Thousands used Hatteras safely as a navigational aid, but between 1526 and 1945 a total of 639 ships perished in storms, hung on sand bars, or foundered in the shallows. Houses in every Outer Banks community utilized the timbers of wrecked ships, and many present-day inhabitants can trace their origins to shipwreck survivors.

The North Carolina coastline attracted lawless men as well. No Charleston or Norfolk sheltered a protecting navy. England authorized privately-owned vessels to attack the Spanish and French, and "privateering" was widely practiced along the Carolina coast. Many English privateers turned to piracy once Queen Anne's War ended, and they found the barrier islands of the North Carolina coastline a perfect place from which to venture into the shipping lanes in search of victims of all nationalities. In 1713, the kingpin of pirates, Edward Teach, or Blackbeard, began a five-year reign of terror along the Atlantic coast, from Virginia to Honduras. He brazenly anchored in Ocracoke and other busy ports, fearing no one. Cavalier in spirit, he donated stolen books to the library in Bath and sold plundered goods to grateful colonists who despised the British navigational laws and tariffs and resented the wealthy Old World shipping companies. In 1718 Governor Spotswood of the crown colony of Virginia determined to end Blackbeard's raids on shipping. He sent a force of marines under the command of Robert Maynard to intercept Blackbeard, and the pirate died during the battle after sustaining 25 wounds. Maynard mounted Blackbeard's head on the bowsprit of his ship for the victorious voyage back to Virginia.

NORTH CAROLINA DIV. OF ARCHIVES & HISTORY

As colorful as Blackbeard's career was that of Stede Bonnet, a British army officer who lived in Barbados in retirement, in a fine home, enjoying high status in the community. Apparently just for the thrill of it, he joined Blackbeard's crew and found piracy immensely to his liking. He fitted out his own ship and began plundering sailing vessels along the South Carolina coast from his own base of operations at the mouth of Cape Fear, near the present site of Wilmington. In a scene remarkably similar to the showdown between Blackbeard and Maynard, Stede Bonnet met defeat at the hands of Colonel William Rhett. He was hanged in Charleston, South Carolina, along with 49 other "Carolina pirates," during the winter of 1718.

Diamond Shoals, ever living up to its deadly reputation, hid German submarines during World War I. They left the Diamond Shoals lightship unmolested at anchor, possibly to avoid scaring Allied ships. After watching a number of vessels be torpedoed, the lightship captain began to "wireless" messages to approaching ships, warning them of the

MICHAEL HALMINSKI

submarines. On August 8, 1918, a U-boat finally torpedoed the Diamond Shoals lightship.

All along the Outer Banks, Coast Guard stations housed men who pulled heavy wooden boats on carriages into the surf, then rowed through the breakers into the stormy sea to save shipwreck victims. The stories of heroism are too many to list here. However, during World War I, the men of the Chicamacomico Station performed a rescue that stands alone in terms of bravery. With German submarines sinking hundreds of Allied ships off the east coast, the morning of August 16, 1918 brought the sound of yet another exploding tanker. John Allen Midgett and six experienced men headed out through the breakers. The British tanker, *Mirlo*, laden with gasoline, had turned the sea into a lake of fire. One large lifeboat full of survivors rowed clear of the flames, but 16 men clinging to another lifeboat slowly roasted alive as their oarless boat drifted helplessly in the center of the lake of flames, in a narrow corridor of open water. They survived the heat as long as they could by holding their breaths and ducking underwater, but one by one, 10 of them tired and slipped beneath the waves. Captain Midgett saw the boat with the six men clinging to it when the wind cleared away the smoke momentarily. Without hesitation he threaded the narrow corridor of open water to pluck the men from the sea.

As he turned to leave he spied a last lifeboat where 19 survivors huddled, blackened and burned, even closer to the flames. The lifeboat itself was burning above the water line and the flesh of the men was singed. Midgett piloted his craft along the very edge of the wall of flames to pull alongside the burning lifeboat and throw them a tow rope. Only 10 of the *Mirlo*'s crew of 54 perished, thanks to Midgett's work that day.

Burned themselves, Midgett and his six surfmen received gold Lifesaving Medals from the U.S. government and Victory Medals from the British government. They also proved the unstated credo of the Outer Banks Life Saving Service: no sea is too rough, no situation too dangerous to deter the long surfboats and their men at oars.

Above: *U.S. Lifesaving Service Station at Cape Lookout.*
Left: *A crew at Swansboro Lifesaving Station.*

Facing page: *Ocracoke lighthouse's stair spiral.*

Ocean and Estuary

CHIP HENDERSON

Above: *The state once hampered by having no ocean port now boasts busy cargo-loading facilities such as this one.*

Standing at the ocean's edge on the Outer Banks near Nag's Head, one actually stands nearly 20 miles out at sea, for the thin strand of sand forms a catwalk that curves away from the mainland to within 10 miles of the Gulf Stream. The environment, more maritime than mainland, attracts those who feel the pull of the ocean, of wildness, of solitude. Here are more miles of protected national seashore than any other eastern state can claim, more than 120 miles of Hatteras and Ocracoke islands and Core Banks, protected from beach to sound, covered in wax myrtle, bayberry, yaupon and salt-meadow cord grass.

When visitors could walk to the top of the Hatteras lighthouse, many were dismayed when they saw the dark Atlantic to the east and vast Pamlico Sound to the west, three times as large as Washington State's Puget Sound. They stood on the merest curving finger of sand, which is regularly overwashed by hurricanes in summer and northeasters in winter. Yet the barrier islands of North Carolina endure, actually moving inland with the rising sea. Once they stood 50 miles east of their present location.

They have seen great change. Here huge windmills once turned grist mills to grind corn and wheat for the early colonists. Land-based whaling stations at Cape Lookout sent boats in search of whales. Here, during the Civil War, the Confederate Navy deposited soldiers to engage the Union forces at Fort Hatteras on the very beach where tourists now sunbathe. More recently, the banks have been proven the most diverse sport and commercial fishery on the east coast. Vacationers find the banks' wildness and beauty irresistible. Outside the boundaries of the national seashore, land prices have soared to $3,000 per beach foot. Developers battle environmentalists over some of the most fragile and complex coastal habitat on earth, for tourist dollars bring more wealth than the early outerbankers ever could have imagined.

In the early 1980s, as the noose of development closed around the best remaining maritime forest on the east coast, The Nature Conservancy designated Nag's Head Woods its top national priority. When representatives from Mobil Oil Company spoke in March 1989 to Manteo area residents on the environmental impact of exploratory wells for natural gas deposits off Cape Hatteras, the oil company speakers had to compete with Greenpeace's smoke-belching scale model of an oil derrick parked just outside on a flatbed truck, blaring a recording of an oil rig's noisy operation. In places on North Carolina's coastline, particularly south of Morehead City, motorists must drive for miles before finding a beach access between cottages and condominiums. Four of the state's five fastest-growing counties are on the coast. Yet on the same coastline, miles of protected seashore allow the most-reclusive, most-demanding naturalist to stand among dunes on the wildest seashore of the east coast. Conflict shapes life on the Outer Banks, pitting man against nature, and rugged individuals against each other.

Most of the original settlers, known as "bankers," were squatters or fugitives or runaway indentured servants, and they seldom left the splendid isolation of their barrier islands to venture inland. Some even had landed after surviving shipwrecks. They lived by fishing, hunting ducks and geese, and farming small plots of land. They kept a watchful eye on the sea, ever hopeful that some bounty might wash ashore. At times they were accused of actually causing shipwrecks by hanging lanterns from the necks of grazing ponies at night. As the feeding animals moved slowly about in the sea-oats and beach-grass of the edge of the dunes, the bobbing lanterns must have looked exactly like the cabin lights of anchored ships. The vessels, lured by the false promise of safe anchorage, confidently rode to their doom.

In the mid-1700s, a representative of the royal colony of North Carolina described the bankers as "a set of people who are very wild and ungovernable, so that it is seldom possible to Execute any Civil or Criminal Writ among them." To the colonists in Virginia—who considered their colony the fifth country of Great Britain, equal to England, Scotland, Wales and Northern Ireland, so close was its tie—North Carolina in general, the Outer Banks in particular, blemished the face of the New

Left: Cape Lookout National Seashore.
Below: At Cape Hatteras National Seashore.

*Confederate artillery, the
Armstrong Battery, at Ft. Fisher.*

whaling vessels operating offshore. However, by the 1879 season whalers took only about four whales annually, averaging 1,800 gallons of oil and 550 pounds of whale bone each, for a total catch value of $4,500.

According to David Stick's book *The Outer Banks of North Carolina*, the bankers named storms, shipwrecks and even whales by association. The "Little Children" whale surfaced when most of the adults were away and young boys took the oars of the whale boats. The Sheep Storm of the 1880s drowned many sheep. In December 1902, the Olive Thurlow Storm wrecked the ship *Olive Thurlow*. In 1933 the Jimmy Hamilton Storm drowned Jimmy Hamilton. In March 1962, the "Ash Wednesday Storm" covered parts of Highway 158, under three feet of water.

Many early bankers worked for the U.S. Lifesaving Service, predecessor of the Coast Guard. The surfmen patrolled the shoreline of Pamlico and Albemarle sounds as well as the ocean beyond the barrier islands, and some fishermen considered the sounds more dangerous than the sea. For 80 winters, men walked the lonely beach patrols on foot, around the clock, watching for ships and fishermen in distress.

The colliding currents off Hatteras, as if they weren't dangerous enough, join forces with a phenomenon called the Hatteras-style low pressure system. Hatteras' extremely violent weather patterns combine warm low-pressure troughs with cold-air masses that build up on the eastern side of the Appalachians, releasing enormous energy.

In the continental U.S., no coastline except Florida's endures as many hurricanes as North Carolina's. Yet most experts agree that these pose less danger to bankers than the winter "north-easters" that can form in fewer than 12 hours and overwash parts of the banks, submerging Highway 12 before residents can flee.

When I spent a week on the Outer Banks in March 1989 to reacquaint myself with the beaches I knew as a child, a northeaster blew for five days, washed five cottages out to sea, damaged approximately 70 others, and heavily eroded the dunes and beaches. The wind blew furiously, making it nearly impossible to walk. Foam billowed a yard deep on the beach and whisked like confetti over the dunes. I sat under a gazebo near the Avalon fishing pier in Nag's Head and watched the storm waves sweep through the pilings of the pier. As they slammed into the base of the dune where the gazebo was located, I could soon see exposed timbers. Within an hour the gazebo stood nakedly on stilts, the sand underneath quickly removed by wave action. The next morning, the gazebo—which could have seated a dozen people easily—had vanished without a trace, claimed by the sea. Countless

World. (Remarkably, North Carolina's first governor, William Drummund, had been hanged for participating in Bacon's Rebellion in Virginia in 1676, after his service in North Carolina.)

The first bankers arrived during the reign of Queen Elizabeth I, and occasionally to this day their descendants use an expression or a word from four centuries ago. In Jonathan Leonard's excellent book *Atlantic Beaches*, he describes his experiences on North Carolina's Outer Banks in 1981. At one point, an old banker told him he took his yaupon tea "reverent." Leonard later looked up the word to find that during Elizabethan times, "reverent" had meant "pure," or in this case without cream and sugar.

From the first, the Outer Banks relied on whaling, as indicated by the 1757 land deed to Joseph Morss and Edward Fuller from John Shackleford, which guaranteed them the right "to fish and whale..." Until after the Civil War, the area supported shore-based whaling operations as well as New England

Sand dunes and sea oats at Cape Hatteras National Seashore.

hot-water heaters bobbed in the foamy surf. I watched an entire shingled roof move rapidly down the coastline among the breakers.

When the great gyre of counterclockwise air that forms a hurricane moves into the vulnerable North Carolina coastline, its spinning northern arm strikes first with winds blowing from the east. During this phase of the storm, the winds literally blow the water out of the sounds on the west side on the barrier islands, and inland into the marshes and creeks of the mainland side of Albemarle and Pamlico sounds. Except for the 120-mile-per-hour winds, a person could stroll half a mile into the sound at this point without stepping into water.

However, when the hurricane eye, or center, passes over the Outer Banks, the wind dies to a dead calm. Jan DeBlieu's book *Hatteras Journal*, one of the best accounts of life on the Outer Banks, describes how her friends who did not leave Rodanthe on Hatteras Island during a hurricane, walked outside as the eye passed. They could see stars overhead. When the eye passes, the storm resumes, with winds now approaching from the opposite direction.

Sharks, sea turtles and seaweed all were harvested by the bankers.

"Post mill" type windmill near Cape Hatteras.

NORTH CAROLINA DIV. OF ARCHIVES & HISTORY

One can only admire the spirit of the early bankers, who endured isolation and adversity, winter storms and hurricanes, and who probably would have lived nowhere else. As in the mountains of North Carolina, a powerful sense of community bonded them, a fraternal order of stout-heartedness. The stovepipe hat rebellion provided a notable, if less than serious, example.

Beaver hats had been in demand for two centuries, but by the 1860s they were out of fashion, replaced by the silk hat from France. Two enterprising merchants bought 10,000 of the obsolete beavers cheaply and loaded them on a little steamer, the *Flambeau*, intending to ship them to South America where demand continued. The *Flambeau* ran aground near Oregon Inlet (which in those days migrated southward at the rate of 82 feet per year) and quickly broke up in rough seas. The Hatteras beaches swam knee-deep in beaver hats, and every man, woman and child on the banks soon owned several. The stately headwear was suddenly very much in style among the bankers, who cared little for fashion. Captain Bannister Midgett said that even the porpoises wore beaver hats that spring. The brief extravagance on the austere banks ended when soldiers of the triumphant Union army searched house by house for the merchants' property, and actually arrested some bankers for their "treasonable thievery."

The bankers lived with the wind, and its working potential was not lost upon them. During the 1700s and 1800s, at least 155 windmills spun on the Outer Banks and in the tidewater region. Probably that many more fell into neglect and disappeared before they were documented. In the book, *The Long Roll*, by a soldier who was part of the Union occupation force of North Carolina's coastal region during the Civil War, Charles Johnson wrote that he was astonished by the number of windmills along the northern part of the North Carolina coastline. Most widely used during the 1880s, windmills rapidly declined near the end of that century as steam- and gas-powered mills and cheap transportation made them obsolete. Most succumbed to severe storms since they strategically occupied the windiest corridors.

The early windmills were ingenious affairs, with arms that could be furled with sails and "reefed" or adjusted so that the amount of canvas suited the wind velocity. If the arms of the windmill turned too swiftly, millstones would scorch the corn meal. A long period of calm, however, might deprive an isolated coastal village of flour or meal. Almost all early mills were "post mills," mounted on large posts with tail poles that could rotate 360 degrees on a metal track so that the sails faced into the wind. The North Carolina mills copied the design used since the 12th century in England. Many large plantations had their own mills. Carteret County boasted nearly half of the known windmills within North Carolina, which itself used more windmills than any other state.

In 1850, the first census on the banks listed these occupations: 48 boatmen and mariners, 22 pilots and five commercial fishermen. At Ocracoke there were 18 seamen, 35 pilots and five commercial fishermen. Only on Hatteras Island was the primary occupation commercial fishing. Pilots guided vessels through the banks' maze of shoals, channels and inlets, but most men relied on commercial fishing for at least part of their yearly incomes. Many independent bankers probably never worked at steady jobs but were jacks of all trades, taking what they needed from the sea, planting crops for their own tables and raising a few cattle for sale. The golden age of commercial fishing arrived after the Civil War and continued until World War II.

Many of the most profitable early fisheries used small boats launched from the beach to encircle schools of fish and deploy nets, which then were pulled by hand onto the beach. Mullet were so plentiful that one haul of a large beach seine might fill as many as 500 barrels. On September 22, 1871, fishermen netted 12,000 barrels of mullet on the North Carolina coast. Bankers bartered salted mullet for corn from the farming communities along the rivers of the Coastal Plain. Shad, which migrate upstream from the sea to spawn, also provided important income—as did the sea turtle, with loggerheads fetching 50 cents each and the small green sea turtles about 15 cents each.

To catch sea turtles, a banker rowed his skiff on the ocean until he sighted a turtle. He tied a rope to his leg and jumped overboard, grabbing the turtle by the shell and steering it toward a shallow area, with the rowboat trailing behind. Upon reaching a sand shoal, the fisherman wrestled the turtle into the skiff.

Bankers hunted the hand-sized diamondback terrapin more intensely than any other species, since gourmets prized the meat for stew. Six-inch females, known as "counts," brought between $30 and $36 per dozen, while the larger males brought as much as $120 per dozen before the Civil War. Fishermen dredged them, caught them in dip nets, dug them from mud banks and even used dogs to locate them by scent. By the Civil War, the diamondback terrapin nearly had vanished.

Oysters were another important cash source and at one time there were serious disputes over oyster beds. The following quote from a letter mailed in 1891 from Roanoke Island, comes from David Stick's book, *The Outer Banks of North Carolina:*

"The people here are poor and depend entirely upon the waters for support, in the way of fishing and oystering. But the Virginia men are down here and have taken entire possession of all the oyster grounds; their boats are much larger than those here, and when these are at work the Virginians will run down upon them and tear them up; and when they try to retaliate it is useless, for they are armed to their teeth with Winchester rifles and some have thirty-six pound guns."

Bankers tried a number of small and unusual commercial fisheries and enterprises over the years. In the 1880s, a porpoise fishery near Hatteras Village harvested from 400 to 500 porpoises per season. The menhaden or "fatback," an important commercial fish for nearly 75 years, provides fertilizer to this day. In 1920, the Ocean Leather Company bought a plant near Morehead City for processing sharks: fins were used in chop suey, skins became leather. In one season, from April to June, fisherman harvested 3,500 sharks greater than six feet long in gill nets.

Bankers harvested even seaweed in the early 1900s. With pitchforks, they harvested eel grass along the shores of Albemarle, Pamlico and Currituck sounds, baled it and sent it to Baltimore, where it stuffed mattresses and cushions. They also found a cash crop in the leaves of the yaupon shrub, which Indians from pre-colonial days had used to make "black tea," and bankers harvested for sale on the North Carolina mainland.

Commercial or "market" hunting of waterfowl was widespread in North Carolina's coastal region beginning in the early 1800s and continuing for about a century. Canvasback ducks brought one dollar a pair, redheads 50 cents a pair and smaller ducks about a nickel apiece. Many men of Currituck Sound made most of their winter income from hunting waterfowl, or from guiding, carving decoys or constructing skiffs for wealthy northerners' shooting clubs. The feats of the market hunters were prodigious and, to sportsmen today, unconscionable. In the 1840s, one man and his two sons on the Outer Banks killed 103 geese in one day, using flint and steel shotguns.

Wind-formed yaupon on Ocracoke Island.

GLENN VAN NIMWEGEN

Two shooters commonly operated from a partially submerged "sink box" blind to kill several hundred ducks in a day, shooting external-hammered double-barrelled ten-gauge blackpowder shotguns with 32-inch barrels. A pair of Chesapeake Bay gunners once killed more than 500 ducks in a single day.

The most highly sought species, the canvasback duck, brought a premium price. The handsome, white-bodied, rust-headed canvasback was so named because the canvas sacks of them shipped to Baltimore and New York from North Carolina's Outer Banks bore the stamp "send canvas back."

News of the sky-blackening numbers of waterfowl along North Carolina's coast gradually reached the cities of the Northeast. Around the middle of the 19th century, wealthy sportsmen from New York, Boston and northern industrial centers began making the arduous journey to North Carolina's Outer Banks by rail, boat and even horse and cart to hunt the seemingly limitless ducks, geese and swans. Prior to 1823, the New Currituck Inlet allowed great volumes of saltwater to enter Currituck Sound, making it primarily suited for oysters and saltwater species. When the inlet closed in 1823, Currituck Sound became primarily freshwater, allowing different species to flourish, including waterfowl and largemouth bass that made the area world-famous among sportsmen. In the decades after the Civil War, wealthy Northerners arrived to find hunting conditions suitable for kings. They bought thousands of acres of beach, island and marsh for as little as 10 cents per acre. By the 1880s, one writer said of the desolate Outer Banks north of Nag's Head, "There is not a foot of this ground in the whole territory that is not owned, registered by title-deeds, recorded in the archives and watched over as if it sheltered a gold mine."

The railroad men and steel men who shot deer in the Adirondacks came to North Carolina's wind-swept coast, modeling themselves after English aristocracy. The Currituck Shooting Club, founded in 1857, became the first of many built by syndicates of sportsmen. Club shares cost from $1,000 to $5,000 or more. Currituck's prime shooting areas were completely tied up by these wealthy sporting fraternities. Curiously, the shooting clubs were not destroyed by the bankers during the Civil War. Northern domination of Currituck's famed shooting ended in the 1920s. Only one clubhouse remains active, the others having been purchased by wealthy individuals or corporations, deeded to conservation groups, or destroyed by storms or fire.

The clubs occupy a special niche in the state's history. The wealthy clubs protected large areas of the Outer Banks from land speculators who developed so much of the North Carolina coastline. Hundreds of thousands of swans, ducks, geese and shore birds still come to North Carolina's brackish-water sounds, many of them now wildlife preserves and sanctuaries.

Orville and Wilbur Wright came to the Outer Banks from Dayton, Ohio at the end of an era. The region was still isolated from the rest of the world. Some of the bankers never set foot on the mainland from birth until death.

Arriving in 1900, the Wrights spent their first year in a canvas tent, shivering in the damp and cold of winter and sweating under wool blankets in spring to escape from mosquitoes. They conducted their experiments with gliders within sight of the ocean, near present Kitty Hawk. In the second year, they built a wooden shack and a small hangar to protect their craft from the endless wind that had enticed them to this remote spot.

Here, they believed, were the ideal conditions to achieve heavier-than-air, or powered, flight. They made more than 1,000 glider flights from the top of a huge sand dune near their camp. Before the Wright Brothers, glider pilots had turned their machines by shifting their weight. The Wrights used cables to curl the wing tips, thus effecting crude ailerons.

They returned to Dayton each year after experimenting with various craft. There in the shop—where they supported themselves on approximately $5,000 per year as bicycle mechanics—they built their own wind tunnel and conducted remarkably precise experiments on leading edges, wing camber and design. Discovering errors in all previous air-pressure tables, they calculated completely new ones and built the world's first aluminum-block engine, which enabled them to build an airplane weighing only 602 pounds. They never accepted any offer of financial assistance.

When the visitor walks the grounds of the Wright Brothers Memorial at Kitty Hawk, it is easy to conjure up images of those bleak years of 1900 through 1904, for the banks still retain much of their wild character. The wind still moans ominously in the winter, the time of the most dependable wind, as it did when the Wrights lived in their wooden shack for months at a time, visiting the men of the nearby lifesaving station when the isolation became too great to endure.

On December 17, 1903, Orville Wright, lying on his stomach on the wing, powered the flying machine down the short, metal track and off the wooden carriage that it rested on. It rose slowly into a strong 27-mile-per hour wind, dipping and rising erratically as he struggled with the controls, and remained aloft for 120 feet, barely a long Frisbee toss. The dedication and persistence of the

Wright Brothers, which allowed neither of them marriage or children, had earned them the mythical ability to fly.

With the approach of the Great Depression, prospects for the Outer Banks and the entire region of Pamlico and Albemarle sounds reached low ebb. Shipwrecks declined and the Lifesaving Service seemed outdated. New laws ended market hunting for waterfowl and reduced bag limits for sport hunting, and declining numbers of water fowl wounded the elite shooting clubs. No ship-building invigorated the banks, and commercial fishing slumped. The diamondback terrapin was nearly extinct. The shore-based whaling and porpoise seining were finished. Work for the pilots and sea men vanished with the steamboat lines on the sounds and declining maritime traffic. The whaling village of Diamond City was a ghost town and Portsmouth was becoming one. There was no commercial outlet for yaupon and a blight was destroying the eel grass.

However, some men from New Jersey came to Dare County and talked to Wash F. Baum of Manteo, chairman of the Board of Commissioners, about developing the banks as a vacation area. The idea was not new, for colonists from the mainland had visited the Outer Banks for recreation long before the American Revolution.

Above: *A Wright Brothers glider flight at Kitty Hawk.*

Facing page: *Canvasback duck decoys in a state where decoy carvers keep alive a craft that has evolved into an art form.*

Above: North Carolina's coast-line—the "Graveyard of the Atlantic"—claims another victim in 1899.

Facing page: Gulf Stream fishing 10 miles of the North Carolina coast. Only off Florida does the Gulf Stream come closer to the mainland of the East Coast.

They needed a bridge to connect the banks' peerless beaches to the rest of the world. State highway officials informed Baum, when he approached them with the idea, that it would be 50 years before such a bridge could be built. Baum began to look for backers on his own. From a rowboat, Baum and Harry Lawrence took depth soundings all over Roanoke Sound, locating the best place for a bridge.

By 1928 Baum completed his bridge and charged a toll of one dollar. When cars rolled off the bridge onto the Outer Banks, they found nothing but deep ruts in the sand, leading in all directions. However, the bridge had let the genie out of the bottle. By 1931 the state completed a highway through the Nag's Head and Kitty Hawk beach areas. The same year, work on the Wright Brothers Memorial began. In spite of crippling unemployment on the banks due to the Depression, a new era was underway.

In 1933, under the rubric "A Coastal Park for North Carolina," the state created an ambitious rehabilitation plan to restore the bald islands and their barren dunes, eroded by countless storms and overgrazed by cattle. From Oregon Inlet to Cape Lookout, a National Seashore Park eventually protected the wildest, most scenic areas of the Outer Banks. A modern coastal highway, utlizing ferries, connected Beaufort to Nag's Head and opened the reclaimed seashore park to the world. The banks entered the 20th century.

During the first century of colonization, North Carolinians believed that the swamps and marshes that covered so much of eastern North Carolina gave off a poisonous vapor known as "miasma," which caused fever and often death. Physicians called the fever "malaria" and blamed it on decaying vegetable and animal matter in the tepid swamps. Hundreds of people died, slaves and masters alike, never suspecting mosquitoes.

Since people who lived on the Outer Banks usually escaped the fever, even as it raged on the mainland, most people assumed that breathing salt air and bathing in salt water ensured survival from the deadly "bad air." Thus, Nag's Head became a popular "watering place" during the mid-1700s. Other coastal communities had grown up around commercial fishing, whaling, ship-building or shipping naval stores, but Nag's Head specifically developed as a resort.

Development has both benefitted and exploited the Outer Banks. Arguments over which is which illustrate the fact that no one understood natural mechanisms that protected the banks until recently. Sixty years ago, the contours of North Carolina's Outer Banks were far flatter than they are today, little more than well developed shoals, thin and low compared to other barrier islands on the North American coastline. In the 1930s, the state of North Carolina began constructing three parallel lines of ocean-front fences from the Virginia border south to Ocracoke Island, to accumulate sand for dunes. The dunes and a forest of pines planted behind the Wright Brothers Memorial responded dramatically. The dunes achieved a height of 15 feet in a span of a few years and handsome sea oats anchored them in place. However, to the dismay of all, the gently sloping beaches, which had been 150 yards wide before the dunes began to impede "overwash" during storms and shrank to 75 yards in width.

In 1966, the Park Service began pumping sand into the steadily eroding beach areas. After several years of replenishing the sand lost to erosion, the Park Service estimated that the "sand nourishment" program would cost $1,000 per linear foot of shore-line and would have to be repeated every five years. By 1971 the agency spent half a million dollars annually on beaches but was losing at least 10 feet of beach per year. The agency finally decided, when some beaches on Hatteras Island had receded to 30 yards in width, that the large dunes created by the 1930s program were ecologically unsuitable as long as the sea was rising and that barrier islands, in order to survive, had to migrate to the west with the shore line. In September 1973, Park Service officials decided to let nature run its course on the banks, with the exception of Highway 12 and Cape Hatteras lighthouse.

When I was on the banks in March 1989 during a furious northeaster, the dunes resolutely resisted overflow of the ocean, and the erosion into their bases was terrific. In places the surf crashed into the very faces of the dunes, leaving no beach at all during high tide. Now scientists suspect that "overwash" itself maintains wide, gradually sloping beaches such as those that existed before "artificial" dunes. A beach-erosion expert announced over the radio during the storm that he was "proud" that North Carolina now prohibits beach stabilization measures, explaining that as long as the ocean operates according to its own laws, our grandchildren will have broad, gradually sloped beaches to walk.

The Albemarle-Pamlico Sound system recently became the first officially designated "estuary of national concern." While the sounds once teemed with healthy grasses, healthy fish nurseries and abundant marine life, pollution from fertilizer runoff and other sources has reduced populations of blue crab, closed many shellfish areas and, most drastic, caused "red sore disease"—which attacks most species, including the popular largemouth bass—in the Chowan River and Albemarle Sound. Test netting of Atlantic menhaden has produced samples with up to 90 percent infection rates of ulcerated micosis, a skin disease that produces lesions so aggressive that they commonly penetrate the body wall, exposing internal organs. Most fish do not survive the infection, which also afflicts flounder, shad, striped bass, weakfish and spot.

In Manteo, I spoke to a fisheries biologist. He told me that North Carolina's offshore waters had the most diverse fishery on the east coast because the ranges of both northern and southern species overlapped there. He showed me graphs of catch figures for all species over the last decade. Only the big-eye tuna and gray trout catches had increased. All the rest, including flounder, croaker, spot, weakfish, sea bass, swordfish and blue-fin tuna, decreased. Some commercial species were in serious trouble. Big-game species such as blue and white marlin showed steady declines, although anglers still take 1,000-pound fish. But an ominous absence of certain ages of bill fish indicates that "recruitment" into the larger weight classes is not occurring.

Fishermen blame corporate megafarms, timber companies and fertilizer plants that damage the fish nurseries of the estuaries and river mouths. Corporate farms and timber officials claim that

MICHAEL HALMINSKI

Above: *Pier fishing at Nag's Head.*

Right: *Snow geese on Pea Island Refuge, one of the important wintering grounds for migratory birds on the East Coast.*

North Carolina over-fishes and under-regulates its waters. Yet, good fishing news surfaces now and then. Terry Stuart, who runs a bait shop on the Outer Banks, told me of the trend toward catch-and-release fishing. All largemouth bass clubs on the sounds and coastal rivers were returning the fish caught during tournaments. Terry told me that he and every bass fisherman he knows seldom kill bass anymore. He described the ingenious method that deep-sea fishermen off North Carolina's coast use, so they can have their cake and eat it, too. When they catch blue or white marlin, they photograph the fish for a color match, then measure it at critical points and release it into the aquamarine waters of the Gulf Stream. They then substitute a molded fiberglass body for the one that "got away," painted to match the individual fish. The bill fisherman lounges in his living room admiring his trophy while the fish swims somewhere in the Atlantic, perhaps off the coast of Venezuela.

Marlin fishing off the coast of North Carolina is exciting and demanding. When the billfish strikes the bait trailing several hundred yards behind the boat, it knocks the line out of a large "clothespin" on an outrigger pole, allowing the bait to hang motionless as if stunned. The bill fish turns and approaches the bait from behind, the handsome dorsal fin cutting the ocean's surface. The angler in the "fighting chair" waits, watches and hopes. A "take" will give the angler a fight he can remember all winter, yet the fish will live on too.

Farther down the coast, on Bald Head Island, another tiny drama quietly unfolds. North Carolina's premier loggerhead turtle nesting habitat attracts more than a hundred of the giants each summer to lay their eggs in the sands just above the high tide line. By mid-July, the peak of the egg-laying season, 10 or more of the 200- to 300-pound loggerheads may emerge from the waves that wash Bald Head Island nightly, each digging a nest in the sand and depositing approximately a hundred white, ping-pong-ball–sized eggs. Once Virginia's coastline marked the most northerly range of nesting loggerheads, but now North Carolina has that dubious distinction: Virginia's entire coastline was deprived of turtles as their numbers and distribution dwindled to 25 percent of their pre–World War II levels.

On Bald Head Island, The Nature Conservancy conducts a loggerhead protection program along 12 miles of coastline. Each night from late May through September, Cindy Meekins and her interns patrol the beaches of the privately owned island. Before the program, turtle nesting success had declined sharply. Many newly hatched loggerheads fell into deep tire tracks on the beaches and, unable to crawl out, dehydrated there or became food for ghost crabs, a natural predator. Or, the hatchlings, which instinctively head for the brightest horizon, crawled toward the lights of the hotels and private residences. Even when concerned residents placed them by hand in the surf, hatchlings turned and crawled toward the artificial lights with fanatical determination.

The Bald Head Island turtle program is the largest of seven such programs in the state. Residents of the island work closely with the turtle patrol, which digs up all eggs deposited on the narrow, severely eroded beaches to save them from high tides. Turtle nests on private property are removed to a hatchery, while those on the five-mile stretch of coastline within the state park are transferred to nearby dunes.

Jan DeBlieu in *Hatteras Journal* describes a gripping scene on North Carolina's Pea Island where two loggerhead nests have been encircled by wire mesh to protect them from natural predators and to corral the hatchlings until they can be gathered and taken to the Marine Resources Center in Manteo, to be kept for a year and then released. Standing over the turtle nests at midnight, she says:

"I shined the light north, then south. Hundreds upon hundreds of ghost crabs froze momentarily and danced away, as closely packed as a living, moving mat. Their numbers extended as far as I could see in both directions. In the diffused beam their shells appeared very white, like chips of plaster. It was an army of crabs afoot in search of food. I thought of the turtles below the sand, pipping through shells, unfurling their bodies as grains of sand trickled around them. The wire mesh surrounding their nests was the only reason to think they would live longer than two minutes.

"Whatever turtles were still beneath the sands of Pea Island would have to evade a mob of crabs to reach the surf. The odds of breaking through those lines seemed remote, maybe worse than a hundred to one. And ghost crabs were only one of a dozen threats to the remaining clutches."

Pea Island Refuge, on Hatteras Island, is also one of the most important resting areas and wintering grounds for migratory birds on the Atlantic flyway. It is an excellent place to observe wildlife on the Outer Banks. Here, Canada geese, snow geese and whistling swans feed in marshes and uncultivated fields along the highway. Through the open window of a vehicle, with a pair of field glasses, a visitor can watch these noble birds that mate for life. Footpaths through the refuge and observation towers reveal otters, minks, muskrats and nearly every kind of puddle duck and some divers on the numerous ponds. The huge whistlers, with

wing spans well over six feet, fly low enough over the dunes so that the observer can hear the creak and buzz of feathers on the downstroke of the snow-white giants' wings.

On North Carolina's coast, renewed interest in traditional wooden boats came just in time. When gasoline and diesel power arrived, the sharpies, shad boats, Carolina spritsail skiffs, Core Sounders and dozens of other sail-powered rigs were forsaken with all the pragmatism that one might expect from commercial fishermen and working watermen. As the 1980s approached, nearly all who had built or worked these sleek and graceful craft had died, or were too old to ever build again. Since most of the work boats had been built by the fisherman himself, worked hard and then unceremoniously discarded, almost no original boats remained.

The North Carolina Maritime Museum in Beaufort, near Morehead City, saw that a unique part of the state's heritage was

Wooden-boat craftsmen keep the boatbuilding tradition alive through a program of the North Carolina Maritime Museum in Beaufort.

CHIP HENDERSON

Above: *Salt marshes such as this now are being seriously studied, in order to be preserved.*

Facing page: *Aerial view of Cape Hatteras lighthouse.*

had its origin in the sleek, log dugout canoes used by the coastal Indians. Liquor smugglers along the coast during Prohibition preferred shadboats, and the boats were so strong that approximately a dozen hundred-year-old ones still are being used, with motors, by Manteo-area fishermen.

Mark Taylor, in his article "Traditional Boats of North Carolina," which appeared in *North Carolina Wildlife Magazine*, called the classic Carolina spritsail skiff the "mule of the coastal fisherman." A 20-foot spritsail skiff could easily carry several fishermen, a large net, and up to 1,000 pounds of fish, and with center board up this remarkable work boat required only four to six inches of water to float.

Largely because of the work done by the North Carolina Maritime Museum and the interest of coastal boaters, handsome spritsail skiffs and white sharpies—with their high "rocker" (or curve fore and aft) and rounded sterns—dock alongside expensive fiberglass luxury sailboats.

Perhaps the most interesting vessel in North Carolina waters today is the 69-foot, square-rigged sailing ship, the *Elizabeth II*. Berthed at the *Elizabeth II* historic site in Manteo, its design reflects the plans and drawings of Elizabethan vessels that brought Sir Walter Raleigh's colonists to Roanoke Island 400 years ago.

Fishing methods vary along the North Carolina coast. "Headboats" carry as many as 50 sport fishermen at a time to reefs and wrecks far offshore where they lower bait to sea bass and other bottom species. (Interestingly, some of the most productive bottom-fishing sites mark the 53 Allied ships sunk by German submarines off North Carolina's coast during War World II, as well as four German U-boats.) Fishing for blue fish in the surf, as they chase bait fish nearly onto the beach, can be as exciting as any fishing in America. In recent years runs of blues have been plentiful and the size of many individual fish approaches 20 pounds. Speckled trout and other species can be taken from small boats or from the shore in protected waters such as sounds and canals. Sport fishing for big game species including tiger sharks is based from nearly every North Carolina coastal city. Indeed, sharks are so plentiful that they are considered a nuisance to fishermen. For the less adventuresome, there is pier-fishing.

Sailing opportunities in North Carolina's inshore and offshore waters are virtually unlimited, but along North Carolina's entire coastline, the little town of Oriental is the premier location.

Surfing is popular along North Carolina's coastline and the Hatteras area offers the best surfing on the East Coast—as evidenced by the surfboards atop cars arriving from nearly every Eastern Seaboard state. When the winter northeasters blow,

slipping away, and intervened. Researchers interviewing old boat builders discovered that three classic sailing craft either evolved entirely, or were refined and adapted, in North Carolina's coastal waters from the 1700s through the early 1900s: the sharpie, the shad boat and the Carolina spritsail skiff.

A Rhode Islander named George Ives introduced the sharpie to North Carolina and a fisherman in the Beaufort area adopted, adapted and refined it. The craft employed the ancient leg-of-mutton sprit-sail rig that lacked the low-swinging boom that makes sailing so hazardous when changing directions. Since many sharpie fishermen fished alone, hauling nets or tonging oysters, this design quickly grew popular. By the 1880s, Tar Heel coastal fishermen were building sharpies with their own innovations. Schooner-sharpies called "Core Sounders," up to 45 feet long, often sailed from North Carolina to the Caribbean loaded with fish, and returned loaded with sugar, molasses and rum. Efficient and seaworthy, they served into the 1930s.

Another North Carolina design, the shad boat, earned renown for its graceful lines and speed. The shape of these vessels

TOM TILL

surfers in wet suits appear like storm petrels and paddle out into the very roughest breakers, in search of the perfect wave.

The North Carolina coastline, with its Outer Banks discouraging close ties to Europe, created the "Colony Different." Today a different set of dynamics shapes life on the coast. Urban refugees arrive yearly in droves. Compared to the crowded, ruined places they left behind, the coast of North Carolina seems nearly pristine. Yet the bankers, the fisheries biologists, the commercial and sport fishermen, all those who knew North Carolina's coastline 40 years ago, know the region is only a shadow of what it was. Many say that the Oregon Inlet bridge doomed the banks to become just like any other stretch of coastline. In Avon and Buxton, once splendidly isolated, developers have plans for golf courses and exclusive homes that they hope to build just as soon as they can find the technology to pump up more water and treat more sewage.

Jan DeBlieu, in her book *Hatteras Journal*, outlines the problems facing the region.

"Hatteras Island is in the process of being 'discovered.' Its new popularity is bound to drive up the cost of living and the dearness of land.

"In a decade Cape Hatteras may well resemble every other East Coast seaside resort, not only physically, but demographically. It is my fear that the independence and self-reliance—the very spirit that has enabled people here to survive storms and shipwrecks and centuries of isolation will virtually cease to exist. What little spirit remains will be relegated to the rather demeaning category 'colorful' or 'quaint.' The concept of 'island time' will become more a relic of a discarded past, in league with hurricane oil lamps, hand-woven fishing nets, and bags of yaupon tea."

Still, heading from Morehead City north to catch the Cedar Island ferry, one drives through tidal marshes so vast they fill the horizon in every direction. Similarly, driving south on Highway 264 from Manns Harbor to Swan Quarter and on to "Little" Washington (the original city named Washington), salt marshlands extend as far as the eye can see. Every square foot of salt marsh is home for billions of tiny creatures, lichens and many types of algae, some with lifetimes shorter than a single day's tidal cycle. Duke University maintains a modern research center near Beaufort where estuarine scientists study the salt marshes. They are discovering, above all else, the resiliency of the coastal estuaries. According to Courtney Hackney, an insatiably curious salt-marsh scientist with UNC at Wilmington, "we can conceivably screw things up for ten years, and when we finally realize what we're doing wrong, the organisms will all come back."

Above: *Wrightsville Beach sailboaters.*

Facing page: *Ocracoke Island sunrise on the Outer Banks.*

of the Jockey's Ridge sand dune, the tallest in the eastern United States. She stood in front of the blade and refused to move. Her defiance spawned the "People to Preserve Jockey's Ridge" organization. Largely because of her efforts, 400-acre Jockey's Ridge State Park exists today. In 1988, Linda Mizell, a 33-year-old dental hygienist, noticed one day in September a small, unobtrusive newspaper article that said North Carolina had 20 days to prepare its response to a plan by Mobil Oil Corporation to explore for natural gas 47 miles from Cape Hatteras, potentially locating 200 offshore wells there. Mizell knew the wells would flush tons of oily drilling mud into an area thick with the larvae of commercially important fish species. She launched a grassroots movement that formed an organization known as "Lega Sea," which is fighting one of the hottest environmental controversies in the state today. When a 163-acre golf course and housing development threatened Buxton Woods—like Nag's Head Woods, a reservoir of biological diversity—the group known as "Friends of Hatteras Island" formed. Now Buxton Woods is part of the North Carolina Coastal Reserve system. In October 1988 "Friends of Roanoke Island" banded together to prevent development of the historically significant north end of the island.

Currents of emotion like these now ebb and flow along North Carolina's coastline. Meanwhile, a finger of the frigid Labrador Current brings cold water from the north, with a host of cold-water ocean species. The warm Gulf Stream carries subtropical marine species. Life forms, northern and southern, meet at sea and on land to form an oasis of diverse life. Nag's Head Woods may become one of America's most-visited sanctuaries, rivaling the great Audubon preserves at Four Hole Swamp in South Carolina and Corkscrew Swamp in Florida. North Carolinians feel an awakening sense that our coast is too precious to lose.

A cautious feeling of hope pervades the entire coastal region, from Pamlico Sound, with its "red-sore disease" in fish, to contaminated shellfish beds, to the estuary fish nurseries contaminated with fertilizer runoff, from Nag's Head to Morehead City.

During the 1950s and 1960s, the pesticide DDT caused eggshells of ospreys, pelicans and other large birds to thin to the point where they broke during incubation. Brown pelicans disappeared in Texas altogether, and their numbers dropped alarmingly in Louisiana, Florida and South Carolina. Now their numbers are literally soaring. On my last visit, I saw brown pelicans by the hundreds, and osprey nests dot the coastal landscape again, on channel markers and telephone poles and in dead trees.

People of the coastline are taking a stand. In 1973, Carolista Golden discovered a bulldozer beginning excavation at the base

FACING PAGE: PAT COCCIADIFERRO

Portrait of Theodosia Burr

Along North Carolina's Outer Banks, unsolved mysteries and riddles are numerous and the accounts of them, passed down by oral tradition, are spellbinding. A lifesaving crew found one majestic five-masted schooner named the *Carroll A. Deering* stranded on Diamond Shoal, near Cape Hatteras, but could not find a living soul on board, although food still was cooking on the stove. The only living creature aboard was the ship's cat. Another "ghost ship" went down offshore in heavy weather, only to surface a few months later and drift eerily down the coastline for miles before sinking again, as if dissatisfied with its first grave. But probably the most intriguing tale of all is that of the portrait of Theodosia Burr.

On July 11, 1804, in Weehawken, New Jersey, a duel was fought between Aaron Burr, the third vice president of the United States, and Alexander Hamilton, one of the principal figures in founding the nation and a primary architect of its Constitution. Hamilton was mortally wounded in the duel and Burr, although acquitted of murder, became a pariah in the society that once recognized him as a man of wit, charm and promise. Depressed and friendless, he apparently summoned his daughter, Theodosia, to join him in New York. She was one of the most intellectual and beautiful women in America, the wife of Governor Alston of South Carolina. She sailed from Georgetown, South Carolina bound for New York on *The Patriot* in 1812, presumably with a small crew. She never was seen again.

In the winter of 1812 a small pilot boat drifted up on the beach at Kitty Hawk, south of Nag's Head, with all sails set and the rudder lashed in place. The interior of the seaworthy little craft showed no signs of struggle. The silk dresses in the closets were obviously those of a high-born lady. On the wall hung the portrait of a beautiful woman. "Wreckers" who discovered the vessel at the water's edge seized its contents. The picture of the unknown woman hung for 57 years in the Outer Banks home of an illiterate woman. Those involved undoubtedly feared reprisals and said little of the pilot boat.

In 1869, Dr. William G. Pool, a prominent North Carolina physician, while summering at Nag's Head, treated an elderly woman living alone in a crude cabin. To show her gratitude, the old woman, who had no money, offered Dr. Pool her only possession of value, the portrait of an unknown woman which her husband had found in an abandoned sailboat nearly 60 years before. Sometime later, Dr. Pool saw a picture of Aaron Burr. He instantly recognized the likeness to the woman in the portrait. Pool sent photographs of the portrait to relatives and contemporaries of Theodosia Burr, who universally acknowledged that the portrait was indeed hers.

Years later, as two criminals faced execution in Norfolk, Virginia, they testified that they had been part of a pirate crew that boarded *The Patriot* off the North Carolina coast, forcing all on board to "walk the plank." A mendicant made the same confession just before he died in a Michigan poorhouse. The dying man said he would never forget how eloquently Theodosia Burr had pleaded for her life, or how calmly she had accepted her fate as she walked off the plank's end into the ocean. He said that even the hardened crew of pirates admired her courage and he himself never forgot the sight of the exquisitely beautiful face of Theodosia Burr disappearing beneath the waves.

The Coastal Plain

The North Carolina Coastal Plain cradles the state's history, for here the first colonists successfully farmed, raised families and formed communities and villages as they trickled south from Virginia in search of new lands. In the Albemarle region the powerful Tuscarora Indians captured John Lawson, who left one of the earliest accounts of North Carolina in his work, *A New Voyage to Carolina*. Despite his admiration for and defense of the Indians, they killed him, for as the first Surveyor General of the state, he had given away huge tracts of their land.

Spanish privateers captured Brunswick after Queen Anne's War in 1748, only to lose it again to the determined townspeople, who captured a Spanish vessel in the process and sold its contents to build one of the first churches in the North Carolina colony.

At Moore's Creek Bridge near Wilmington, 1,000 patriots defeated 1,600 Tories, primarily Highland Scots, in February 1776. The number of men engaged here more than doubled the forces at the Battle of Lexington and Concord, a year earlier, where colonists fired the "shot heard 'round the world." The Battle of Moore's Creek Bridge became known as "the Lexington and Concord of the South."

Lord Charles Cornwallis, commander of the British forces during the American Revolution, retreated to Wilmington after the Battle of Guilford Courthouse to recover from his losses before marching to Yorktown, where he surrendered.

Beaufort preserves the grave of American privateer Otway Burns. During the War of 1812, when the British Navy blockaded the East Coast, Burns captured so many British merchant ships with his vessel *Snapdragon* that Britain placed a bounty of $250,000 on his head.

Early in the Civil War, the Federals occupied parts of the Coastal Plain—"Little" Washington, for example, in March 1862. Confederate efforts to retake "Little" Washington nearly destroyed it. The Roanoke Island fortifications fell to Federals in February 1862 after a naval battle, when 7,500 Union soldiers under General Ambrose Burnside stormed the island. Fort Macon,

near Morehead City, fell a short time later after sustaining 560 direct hits from Union naval vessels. Confederate guerrillas blew up both Bodie Island Lighthouse and Cape Lookout Lighthouse in an attempt to hinder Union shipping.

The port of Wilmington at the mouth of Cape Fear, defended by powerful Fort Fisher, "the Gibraltar of America," held out nearly to the end of the Civil War, withstanding Federal attacks in 1862 and 1864. It was the most important fort for blockade runners, who carried half the food for the Confederate army during the last years of the war. After materials arrived in Wilmington, the South shipped them to the battlefields of Virginia by way of the Wilmington and Weldon Railroad, the "Lifeline of the Confederacy." The fall of Fort Fisher and Wilmington in January 1865 sealed the fate of Lee's army

Only one other significant battle took place on North Carolina's soil, the battle of Bentonville, fought 17 days after Lee's surrender to Grant at Appomattox Courthouse. The battle inflicted 2,606 Confederate and 1,646 Union casualties.

As the deepening gloom of the Civil War approached, the election of 1860 showed that the overwhelming majority of North Carolina voters were Unionists opposed to secession. But President Lincoln's demand for troops from all the Southern states to quell the rebellion in South Carolina did more than all the secessionists to break up the Union. "North Carolina would have stood by the Union, but for the conduct of the National Administration…which for folly and simplicity exceeds anything in modern history," future governor Jonathan Worth said in May 1861.

Once committed to the Confederacy, North Carolina provided more soldiers to its army than any other state. Tar Heels said they were "First at Bethel, Farthest to the Front at Gettysburg and Chickamauga, Last at Appomattox." With only one ninth of the Confederacy's population, it suffered more than one fourth of Confederate battle deaths. The 26th North Carolina Regiment suffered casualties of 86 percent at Gettysburg, more than any other regiment on either side. Eleven Civil War battles and 73 skirmishes were fought within North Carolina's borders.

Above: *Scottish Highlander.*

Facing page: *Winter sunset.*

Some residents of mountain and Piedmont counties took anti-slavery stands and fought for the Union. Surprisingly, although the mountains were not noted for agriculture, in 1850, in Buncombe, Burke, Caldwell, McDowell and Rutherford counties, slaves constituted nearly 20 percent of the total population. After the Civil War, some Piedmont and mountain families changed the spellings of their names to separate themselves from the "traitors" who fought for the Union.

The history of the Coastal Plain offers other fascinating glimpses of life long ago. The celebration of Jonkonnu among slaves may well be the most unusual. Slavery was practiced most widely on the huge plantations of North Carolina's flat Coastal Plain. Here, from Fayetteville east to the coast, planters feared Christmas celebrations among slaves. Taking advantage of their masters' benevolent mood, slaves made demands of the planters, even mocked them. On many the plantations in the eastern part of the state, normally docile slaves appeared each Christmas, dressed in colorful costumes, beating drums, some wearing white makeup, men dressed as women and women dressed as men. They would walk to the planter's front porch and shout for him to come out. They demanded liquor, money or gifts. A slave even might stride up the porch steps and shake the master by the hand. In extreme cases slaves demanded to enter the planter's home and go from room to room. Masters who refused found themselves the butts of mocking, insulting songs. Elizabeth Fenn, of Hillsborough, whose research turned up this fascinating North Carolina history, interprets Jonkonnu as release for the enormous frustration and resentment slaves felt towards their masters. While the tradition of Jonkonnu gained wide acceptance in the Caribbean, apparently the only U.S. state to tolerate it was North Carolina, the "Colony Different."

Wilmington, more than 250 years old and until 1910 the state's largest city, preserves a long history rich in more conventional forms of entertainment. Thalian Hall, built in 1858 and originally lighted by 188 gas burners. Tyrone Power, 19th-century actor and student of theater architecture (great-grandfather of the namesake film actor), once said, "I think there are three great theaters in the world, the Drottingham Royal Palace near Stockholm, built in 1764; the Theatre Royal (Old Vic), Bristol, England in 1766; and the Thalian Hall, Wilmington, North Carolina." Many greats have walked the boards of the Thalian, from Tom Thumb to Oscar Wilde. Thalian Hall is widely recognized for its acoustics. Lawrence Tibbett, a Metropolitan Opera star, remarked after a concert at the Thalian Hall that its acoustic properties were among the finest he had encountered. Huge crowds came here on the eve of the Civil War to hear speakers debate North Carolina's secession. Union troops patronized Thalian Hall during the last year of the Civil War, after the fall of Fort Fisher. Not only is Thalian Hall home to the oldest little-theater association in America, but Thomas Godfrey wrote the first play in America, *The Prince of Parthia*, in 1763 in Wilmington.

Numerous grand antebellum residences and plantation homes still stand in Wilmington, and some such as Orton and Airlie feature public gardens and offer blooming schedules for their azaleas, camellias, wisterias, hydrangeas, magnolias, crepe myrtles and many other species.

In addition to these, Venus's fly-traps, a unique insectivorous plant, may be seen in the trail area of Carolina Beach State Park. For the student of literature, in nearby Southport is the house where Robert Ruark grew up, having the experiences with his grandfather, riverboat Captain Edward Hall Adkins, which he would write about in *The Old Man and the Boy* and *The Old Man's Boy Grows Older*.

Tourists ride horse-drawn carriages to Wilmington's historic downtown district and board the *Henrietta II*, modeled after the 19th-century paddlewheeler *Henrietta*, which ran the Cape Fear River for 40 years. The *Henrietta II* carries visitors on 90-minute day cruises and leisurely dinner cruises at night during the summer.

The city of Wilmington, the state's only world-class port, accommodates vessels from all over the earth. Anchored permanently in Wilmington is the 36,300-ton U.S.S. *North Carolina*, which once carried a crew of 2,000 and participated in every major Pacific naval campaign in War World II, from Guadalcanal to Okinawa. A self-guided tour of the ship takes two hours and, in the summer, sound and light shows are held every two hours. The *Northwind*, the nation's largest icebreaker and veteran of many Bering Sea patrols, calls Wilmington home port and is open to the public.

North Carolina's colorful, unconventional movie-making history surprises even many Tar Heels. In 1921, the state pioneered educational films with a five-reel study of the Lost Colony filmed on Roanoke Island. Financed by the North Carolina Historical Commission and the State Board of Education, the project used more than 200 actors, and sets produced on location. It played all over the state and, where no electricity was available, Model T Fords generated power.

During the 1930s, North Carolina's film industry depended on two colorful promoters, H. Lee Waters of Lexington and

Holly Smith of Charlotte. Waters visited North Carolina towns and filmed local people at their daily activities, then returned with the finished film a few days later to show the townfolk, for a small fee. His beautifully shot, silent documentaries, often 90 minutes long, preserve an easygoing lifestyle and gentle friendliness. He made more than 252 films in 117 towns, mostly in North Carolina. Most of Waters' films have vanished, but the North Carolina State Archives owns 14.

Holly Smith used the "see-yourself-in-pictures" idea too, but his films featured local businesses. Smith was the first Tar Heel to use sound with film, and some of his work—rare footage of bright-leaf tobacco auctions in 1948 in Wilson, cotton ginning, car lots selling the latest Packards and DeSotos—speaks eloquently of a bygone era.

Earl Owensby of Shelby, another self-styled promoter, has written a chapter of North Carolina film history around his childhood dream of becoming a movie star. He began his career selling pneumatic tools out of the trunk of his car and did so well

Above: *The U.S.S.* North Carolina *battleship is permanently moored in Wilmington*

Facing page: *Barrels of turpentine destined for explort from Wilmington harbor, now North Carolina's only world-class port.*

that he soon became president of his own company. Next he built a $5 million film studio and began to crank out such titles as "Man Hunter," "Death Driver," "Dark Sunday," "Buckstone County Prison"—all starring Earl Owensby. Owensby's recurrent speed and violence themes proved popular; none of his movies has lost money.

The most recent chapter of the North Carolina movie saga was written when Italian producer Dino De Laurentiis, the producer of such movies as "La Strada" and "Ragtime," moved to Wilmington. He quickly built a huge and very expensive film studio, reputably one of the largest in the world, and filmed "Firestarter" and "Blue Velvet." Wilmington, for a brief time, harbored fantasies of becoming the Hollywood of the East Coast, but De Laurentiis filed bankruptcy within a few years and the corporation became the North Carolina Film Studios Incorporated.

North Carolina's non-union workforce, unbeatable scenery and "can do" attitude have lured other producers. So far, 140 films shot partially or totally within the state have added $99 million direct revenue for the state and $297 million in economic impact. such popular movies as "Bull Durham," "Dirty Dancing," "The Color Purple," "Everybody Wins," "The Winter People," "Crimes of the Heart" and "Being There" were filmed in North Carolina.

The North Carolina Coastal Plain, unlike the nearby frantic coastline, slumbers much as the mountains do. Its battlefields are silent now and the area attracts attention chiefly as a wine-producing region, a "sleepy hollow" where historic colonial homes are open to visitors, and the site of world-class golf courses in Pinehurst and Southern Pines. Yet the flat, black-earth region also supports thriving truck farms that harvest cotton, corn and Irish and sweet potatoes. Faison, with a population of 600, located near Goldsboro, boasts the second-largest vegetable exchange in the nation. Buyers ship North Carolina Coastal Plain vegetables from tiny Faison by truck and rail as far away as Canada, Chicago and Detroit. Nearby farms produce 400,000 bushels of cucumbers yearly, many of which end up as Mount Olive pickles packed in nearby Mount Olive. This is fabulous hog country, with its Smithfield hams recognized nationally.

Bright-leaf tobacco "lots," piled in shallow baskets and arranged in rows in huge warehouses, bring auctioneers and buyers who judge color, texture and aroma and make purchases with unintelligible chatter and subtle gestures. Wilson, Rocky Mount and Kinston have some of the world's largest tobacco markets. One such market requires a total floor area of 53 square acres.

Underscoring the importance of tobacco in the Coastal

Plain, Kenly, just east of Raleigh, displays early leaf farming equipment and tools in its Tobacco Museum.

The Coastal Plain is an area where peanut fields extend out of sight. Of the 1 billion pounds of goobers Americans eat yearly, North Carolina grows nearly one third.

In the ancient Albemarle region, picturesque bridges span inland arms of Pamlico and Albemarle sounds. According to a government survey, Dare County, including its ocean coastline, inland sounds, and fresh and brackish water bodies, contains more species of fish than any other county in America, from the prehistoric long-nosed gar and brindle, or "blackfish," to the highly-prized striped bass.

In a curious echo from history, the same area where planters owned huge plantations now features cultivated tracts of land so large that they required a new term: "megafarm." Corporations have bought much of the Albemarle-Pamlico Peninsula. In 1972, John Hancock Mutual Insurance Company and American Cyanamid bought 35,000 acres of Albemarle-Pamlico. Japanese and Italian interests bought 50,000 acres here two years later. In 1975, McLean Trucking bought 374,000 acres, or one third of the entire peninsula, and named its holdings "First Colony Farms." That same year, John Hancock Mutual Insurance bought yet another 26,000 acres. These corporate giants have cleared vast stands of swamp forest and pocosin. They have mined peat for conversion to methanol fuel. They are farming row crops, relying heavily on fertilizer that runs off into Pamlico Sound. In 1981 a Duke University ecologist and two colleagues revealed that 70 percent of pocosins in the United States occur in North Carolina and that between 1962 and 1979, timber companies entirely cleared one third of the them and partially cleared another 36 percent. Only five percent were within state and federal preserves. In the last 10 years ecologists and marine scientists have learned that the freshwater swamps and pocosins play a critical role in controlling runoff into the rivers and vast Pamlico and Albemarle sounds, which once teemed with fish, crab and shrimp. Conservation groups now fear that North Carolina pocosins are becoming farmland so rapidly that Albemarle Sound may never recover.

Yet while the Albemarle-Pamlico Peninsula is undergoing change, much of the Coastal Plain offers the visitor a calm from centuries ago. Bath, the oldest town in the state and its first official port of entry, is where the first colonial assembly convened. The colonial atmosphere has not been surrendered, and some homes, old even before the American Revolution, are open to visitors.

New Bern, the second-oldest town in the state, had a stormy early history. With instructions to create a town and name it after Bern, Switzerland, two ships with 650 German and Swiss passengers and a few English left Europe in 1710. A French man-of-war captured one of the vessels in the Chesapeake Bay. Storms and disease ravaged the other ship. Later the same year, another 156 Swiss arrived, accompanied by Baron Christoph de Graffenreid. John Lawson surveyed the town, laying it out in the shape of a cross. The infant town endured savage attacks by Tuscarora Indians, including one on September 22, 1711, that slaughtered 130 people in North Carolina's worst carnage of the entire colonial era. In 1713, many of the Swiss returned to Europe with de Graffenreid, who had been a Tuscarora hostage for six months. The village gradually grew and developed a gay social life, with horse-racing tracks, fox hunts and lavish balls. A

Above: Tobacco warehouse scene.

Facing page: Tobacco has been North Carolina's top cash crop from colonial times to the present.

brisk shipping trade, carried on with light, shallow-draft vessels, supplied the New England ports of Boston and Salem with leaf tobacco, molasses, lumber and naval stores.

In New Bern, "Tryon's Palace" (completed in 1770), was considered the finest "House of Government" in the English colonies. Colonists in the western counties greatly resented poll taxes levied to finance it. The Orange County farmers wrote in 1768, regarding the governor's mansion, "We want no such House, nor will we pay for it."

Tryon's Palace, now open to the public, features colonial children's games, and special events during the Annual Tryon's Palace Colonial Living Day in May and at Christmastime.

Edenton, the third-oldest oldest town in the state, served at the western end of Albemarle Sound for nearly 40 years as the unofficial capital of the colony. The Edenton Tea Party, held by the women of Edenton to protest the Tea Act of 1773, marked the first political action by women in the American colonies. Edenton shipped relief supplies to Boston in the summer of 1774, when the port was closed after the Boston Tea Party.

Once herring and shad provided the economic mainstay of Edenton, but the decline of the Albemarle and Pamlico sound fisheries has shifted emphasis to agriculture. The jumbo peanut thrives in the fine, loamy soil of the region.

To the modern traveler acquainted with North Carolina's comfortable, intimate bed-and-breakfasts, an English traveler's account of the "Carolina Ordinary" in colonial times sounds almost unbearable:

"They were mostly log-huts, or frame weatherboarded…the more numerous having no internal divisions…One corner of the room would be occupied by a 'bunk' containing the family bed…The rest of the furniture consisted of two chairs and a table, all in the last stage of palsy…If hunger and fatigue compelled you to remain, a little Indian corn for your horse, and a blanket on the hearth, with your saddle for a pillow, to represent a bed, were the most you could obtain…As to edibles, whether you called for breakfast, dinner, or supper, the reply was one—eggs and bacon…Ten to one you had to cook the meal yourself…The young children, never less than a dozen, (the women seeming to bear them in a litter in these regions) at the sight and smell of victuals would let up a yell enough to frighten the wolves."

Manteo, on the edge of the coastal estuary and the Coastal Plain, stages the nation's oldest outdoor drama, based on Pulitzer-Prize–winning dramatist Paul Green's 1937 work, *The Lost Colony*. Other Coastal Plain productions include "First for Freedom" (Halifax), "Strike at the Wind" (Pembroke) and "The

Liberty Cart" (Kenansville). In fact, no other state presents as many outdoor dramas as North Carolina. An Institute of Outdoor Drama at University of North Carolina at Chapel Hill testifies to the popularity of this art form in the Tar Heel State.

In the mountains, "From This Day Forward," presented in Valdese, depicts the struggles of members of the Waldenses Church in the Blue Ridge Mountains. "Horn in the West" in Boone, which has run for 36 successive seasons, tells of the struggle of Daniel Boone and the Mountain Men against the British and Indians during the American Revolution. "Unto

The Coastal Plain's "up country" supports a thriving wine industry that dates from German and Swiss vintners of the early 1700s.

Left: *A restored colonial home in Old Salem.*

Facing page: *A scene from "The Lost Colony," the outdoor drama recounting the story of the first permanent English settlement in the New World.*

61

CHIP HENDERSON PHOTOS

These Hills," in Cherokee, is the story of the Cherokee Indians as they were forced out of the mountains and sent on the Trail of Tears to Oklahoma.

The Piedmont section of the state has "The Sword of Peace" in Snow Camp, the story of Quakers' peaceful resistance during the American Revolution. "Listen and Remember," presented in Waxhaw, tells the history of the region south of Charlotte through revolutionary times.

The Coastal Plain's Intercoastal Waterway winds through the tidewater, following the natural sounds and rivers or flowing straight as an arrow through a canal in the low country. The Intercoastal Waterway, utilizing old canals and other waterways, makes possible an inland passage of 3,000 miles, from Boston to Brownsville, Texas. The North Carolina section ranks as one of the wildest, most interesting stretches, used each year not only by commercial traffic but also by the migratory folk who summer in New England and winter in Florida. Many of the tidewater towns along the Intercoastal Waterway cater to these travelers as they pass through the state.

Lake Waccamaw may be one of the most biologically unusual water bodies in the nation. Like Russia's Lake Baikal, Lake

Tanganyika in Africa and the volcanic lakes of the Philippines, Lake Waccamaw contains many endemic fauna, fishes, mollusks and crustaceans, which are restricted to the lake and found nowhere else. In the clear, spring-fed waters of this largest "Carolina Bay" (see page 24), a rare process called "speciation" takes place. New species form rapidly from preexisting ones due to isolation from parental stocks, interbreeding and random chromosomal mutations. At Lake Waccamaw, which is only a few thousand years old, researchers already have distinguished four species from their parent species still teeming in the nearby lowland streams. The Waccamaw shiner, the Waccamaw darter, the Waccamaw killifish and the Waccamaw silverside occur nowhere else in the world.

The red wolf, which once ranged from the Atlantic seaboard to Texas and Oklahoma, and north to the Ohio River Valley, disappeared from the wild during the first half of the 20th century. This shy, secretive, gentle, nocturnal animal has escaped total extinction thanks to captive programs in Washington State and other locations. In 1984, the Prudential Insurance Company donated 120,000 acres in Dare and Tyrrell counties to form the Alligator River National Wildlife Refuge. Within the entire historic range of the species, only the Alligator River refuge seems large enough to support the number of family groups necessary to avoid genetic inbreeding.

The Fish and Wildlife Service office in Manteo manages the North Carolina red wolf program. At 9:30 a.m. on September 14, 1987, two adult wolves born and raised in captivity loped onto the Alligator preserve, marking the first time in history that a species extinct in the wild had been returned to its former range.

The "up country" of the Coastal Plain, pervaded by a quiet, almost antebellum graciousness, is home to East Carolina University in Greenville, the largest institution of higher learning in this region. The thriving wine industry here, one of the oldest in the nation, dates to the early 1700s when Germans and Swiss settled the New Bern area. The scuppernong, the nation's oldest commercial wine grape, played a prominent role then and does so now. In Halifax County's Brinkleyville, Sidney Weller founded the nation's first winery, naming it Medoc Vineyard in homage to the wine region of France. He used both muscadines and scuppernongs. Paul Garrett, of Edgecombe County, produced "Virginia Dare" wine, the best-selling wine in the United States before Prohibition. Garrett's five North Carolina wineries made him the state's preeminent wine maker at the turn of the century, although more than 25 others operated in North Carolina at that time.

Today the state supports five wineries and ranks ninth in the nation in wine production. Near the Duplin County town of Rose Hill, 1,500 acres of muscadines dominate the landscape. Duplin's Cellar Winery produces and markets wines exclusively from North Carolina grapes and accepts only grapes delivered to the winery on the same day they are picked. Duplin Cellars boasts customers from all over the nation, and conducts visitor tours.

In the mountains, the Biltmore Estate winery aims to remain medium-sized and produce truly fine wines, priced to sell competitively with California wines: Chateux Biltmore and Biltmore Estates. The winery is open to the public.

In addition to Duplin and Biltmore, there are Carolina Winery, also in Duplin County, Germanton Vineyards and

MICHAEL HALMINSKI

Left: The red wolf, once extinct here, was reintroduced into the Alligator preserve in 1987.

Facing page: Tryon's Palace facade and costumed interpretors at work in the kitchen.

come to North Carolina inspired by a memorable vacation; others move north from Florida because they miss the four seasons. Today's retirees are healthy, well-educated and financially secure. They like North Carolina's mountains, Piedmont and ocean, its culture, and the strength of its service sector. North Carolina has four medical centers compared to Florida's two. The Center for Creative Retirement at Asheville, the only such center in the nation, offers pre-retirement planning, a college for seniors, an adult wellness center, a senior leadership academy, senior service leagues and other services. North Carolina's Elderhostel program, affiliated with the national program, allows adults older than 60 to live in a college dorm, eat in the cafeteria and enroll in college courses. The top retirement areas in the state include the Asheville-Hendersonville-Brevard area, the Triangle, the Sandhills, the Cape Fear Region and the Edenton-Coastal Area.

The Coastal Plain is an area rich in tradition, particularly the Cape Fear River Valley, which was peopled by Highland Scots who continued to speak Gaelic for decades after being allowed to leave Britain following the English defeat of Bonnie Prince Charlie in 1746.

Fayetteville, the population center of the upper Cape Fear region, has shed its reputation as a military-base town and is undergoing a transformation. It recently was awarded All-America City status and has revitalized its many historic landmarks.

North Carolina's Coastal Plain occupies nearly half the state. Overshadowed until now by the famous Outer Banks, the high-energy Piedmont and the forest-covered mountains, the Coastal Plain now is building a reputation of its own.

Above: North Carolina offers some of the world's finest golf courses, as here on Bald Head Island off the coast near Wilmington.
Right: Up and away at the autumn balloon rally at Statesville in the Love Valley.

Facing page: Pinehurst Hotel and Country Club.

Winery in Stokes County, Larocca Wine Company in Fayetteville and Southland Estate Winery near Smithfield.

On the edge of the Coastal Plain, the Carolina Sandhills long have grown peaches. The North Carolina Agriculture Experiment Station here has developed 15 varieties of peaches, 13 of them named for towns in the Sandhills. For North Carolinians, a drive through the Sandhills on the way to the beach has always been an outing in itself, for here groves of manicured, fruit-laden peach trees blow past the open window, mile after fragrant mile.

The Sandhills golf courses equal any in the world. Tournaments here draw the biggest names in golf. Pinehurst Country Club, with its famed Number Two Course, its World Golf Hall of Fame and its 10-foot bronze statue of Bobby Jones, is truly mecca for the golfer.

Many avid golfers are retirees, and North Carolina ranks seventh in the nation in-migration of retirees. Some retirees

James Waddell & the Shenandoah

Facing page: James Waddell, whose ship was the only one ever to bear the Confederate flag around the world.

James Waddell was born in Pittsboro, North Carolina in 1824, a descendant of Hugh Waddell and General Francis Nash, both Revolutionary War heroes. Young James Waddell showed early his Celtic temperament, for at the age of 18, as a midshipman at the Naval Academy at Annapolis in 1841, he challenged an upperclassman to a duel after a heated argument. His opponent was a crack shot, and the ball from his dueling pistol lodged in Waddell's hip. He walked with a slight limp for the rest of his life.

Waddell was serving as an officer in the U.S. Navy when the Civil War broke out. He resigned and reported for duty with the Confederate Navy. His orders were to locate and destroy the U.S. whaling fleet, which supplied oil for the lamps of the Union army and operated in Arctic waters between the Aleutian Islands of Alaska and the Kamchatka Peninsula of Russia. Armed with map, compass and an iron will, James Waddell set out on an odyssey that has few parallels in history.

The Confederate government purchased the vessel *Sea King* in Europe for Waddell's mission. Fitted both with sail and a steam-driven propeller, the teak-hulled vessel accommodated a crew of 150. Waddell sailed a second vessel, the *Laurel*, loaded with cannon and munitions, to the coast of Morocco, where he rendezvoused on October 19, 1864 with the *Sea King*. As the Confederate flag popped and cracked in the North African wind, Waddell re-christened his ship *Shenandoah*.

When Waddell informed the crew of 55 of their objective, 32 men left with the *Laurel*. Waddell and his officers helped pull up the *Shenandoah's* giant anchor, so undermanned were they. The 23 remaining crew and ship's officers set about converting the merchant ship into an armed cruiser, cutting gun ports and portholes and mounting cannons, Waddell working jacketless with the rest.

After a series of easy prizes, the *Shenandoah,* loaded with prisoners from whom came 20 enlistments, rounded the Cape of Good Hope on the southern tip of Africa and continued toward the Orient and Australia. At Melbourne, Aus-tralia, Waddell released his prisoners and enlisted more crewmen, increasing their number to 144, and headed north toward United States whaling fleet. The *Shenandoah* arrived in the Bering Sea between Alaska and the Kamchatka Peninsula of Russia on June 23, 1865.

In search of whalers, the *Shenandoah* sailed so far north that Captain Whittle remarked in his journal, "We went up as far as Gifinski and Tansk Bay, but could not enter the ice, which was from 15 to 30 feet thick. Frequent captures were made, and the smoke of the burning vessels made landmarks against the skies." Here, Waddell and his crew watched the sun drop nearly to the horizon, only to rise again.

In mid-summer Waddell captured two whaling ships that had on board newspapers reporting that Lee had surrendered at Appomattox. But the same issue carried the statement of Jefferson Davis, President of the Confederacy, that Lee's surrender only demanded continuing the war with greater vigor. The dark-hulled *Shenandoah* hunted the Arctic waters relentlessly. Whittle noted in his journal, "Between June 22 and 28 we captured twenty-four whaling vessels, eleven being taken on the 28th." Some of the prisoners, as they watched their ships burn to the waterline, "expressed their opinion" that the war was over, but so great was the charisma of Captain Waddell that eight captives enlisted to serve him, whatever his mission. He continued his attacks as he turned south.

On August 2, the *Shenandoah* overtook a British vessel only 13 days out of San Francisco. From its captain, Waddell learned of the surrender of all Confederate forces, the capture of Jefferson Davis and the collapse of the Confederacy. He learned that federal cruisers were searching for him everywhere. Recent newspapers confirmed it all.

Waddell decided to head for Europe to seek asylum. The *Shenandoah* rounded stormy Cape Horn, at the southern tip of South America, on September 15 and set course for Liverpool, England. "We passed many sails," says Whittle, "but exchanged no signals. We were making no new acquaintances." They crossed the equator for the fourth time on October 11, 1865.

In early November, the *Shenandoah* sailed into the Irish Sea, having navigated 23,000 miles without sighting land. The next morning, November 6, 1865, the *Shenandoah* steamed up England's Mersey River, proudly flying the flag of the Confederacy. Thus, the *Shenandoah* became the only vessel to bear the Confederate flag around the world. In its 13-month cruise, the ship covered 58,000 miles and did not anchor for eight months. The *Shenandoah* destroyed more vessels than any other ship of war except the *Alabama*. It had captured 38 ships, burning or scuttling 32 of them, taken 1,153 men prisoner, and cost the northern maritime industry $1,172,223.

At 10:00 a.m. on November 6, 1865, Waddell lowered the flag of the Confederacy for the last time and turned over the *Shenandoah* to the British government. Waddell remained in Europe for 10 years to avoid retribution. When he died at Annapolis, aged 61 in 1886, the Maryland legislature adjourned for one day in his honor.

Aging Confederate soldiers marched to his home. The Governor of Maryland, a state that had fought for the Union, attended the funeral. Waddell's state funeral was the only one accorded a Confederate in a state north of the Potomac.

NORTH CAROLINA DIV. OF ARCHIVES & HISTORY

Piedmont

Above: Aerial view of the North Carolina State Fair at Raleigh.

Facing page: Raleigh skyline.

While North Carolina's beautiful mountains and Outer Banks offer solitude and inspiration, the state's Piedmont region is the engine that pulled the "Rip Van Winkle State" out of its role as the frontier of Virginia and South Carolina and drew North Carolina into regional prominence. The Piedmont's mold was cast and tempered during the colony's infancy, when the thrifty, hard-working German, Moravian, English and Scotch-Irish arrived with their passionate belief in the dignity of the individual.

The United Brethren followers of John Huss, who was burned at the stake for opposing the Church in the 15th century, had fled from Bohemia into the mountains of Moravia, where they become known as "Moravians." They arrived in the New World and settled where Winston-Salem now stands. The Presbyterian Scots, taxed and tariffed by the English until they fled from the Old World to the colonies, arrived in North Carolina's Piedmont dedicated to the concept of "no taxation without representation." In 1767, North Carolina Royal Governor William Tryon admitted that his "sheriffs" had embezzled all but £500 of the £40,000 in taxes they collected that year, and infuriated the primarily English, German, Scotch-Irish and Moravian colonists. In March 1771, 2,000 "Regulators" opposed 1,452 militiamen under Tryon. Although the regulators lost the battle of Alamance, they showed that the small farmers of the Piedmont were resolved never again to be hounded or taxed mercilessly by any government.

The Piedmont, from the very beginning, valued education highly. In 1767, where Greensboro now stands, David Caldwell opened his Log College, the first institution of higher learning in the state. Young men came to Caldwell's school from every state south of the Potomac. Caldwell's graduates included the most distinguished statesmen, judges, doctors and ministers of their day. Five students became governors: three consecutive governors of Alabama, one of Tennessee, and John Motley Morehead of North Carolina. The British considered Caldwell himself such a threat to their interests that they put a £200 reward on his head,

but he lived to be 99 years old—old enough to turn down an offer of the presidency of University of North Carolina in 1794.

From the Battle of the Regulators at Alamance until the Revolution ended, the Piedmont played an active role in the struggle for democracy. After the Battle of Kings Mountain, where mountain men defeated Colonel Ferguson's force in what many call the turning point of the American Revolution, British and Tory prisoners were guarded in Wachovia, near Salem.

Where Greensboro now stands, its namesake General Nathaniel Green and 4,000 colonists, many of them inexperienced, opposed Lord Charles Cornwallis and his 2,253 seasoned veterans. Cornwallis, a veteran of European wars, said later, "I never saw such fighting since God made me. The Americans fought like demons." While the British held the battlefield, Cornwallis lost 93 killed and 413 wounded, nearly one fourth of his army. But his experienced officers suffered the highest casualties and Charles James Fox said, "Another such victory would destroy the British Army." Cornwallis never recovered from the historic battle of Guilford Courthouse, and he surrendered at Yorktown, Virginia seven months later. The fight-and-retreat tactics of Nathaniel Green worked so well that, in the words of Horace Walpole, "Lord Cornwallis has conquered his troops out of shoes and provisions and himself out of troops." Guilford Courthouse became the nation's first National Military Park.

Following the American Revolution, the social order in North Carolina remained much the same. The University of North Carolina, which first opened its doors to students in 1795 and remained the only institution of higher learning in the state for nearly half a century, offered primarily a "classical school" curriculum, a "gentleman's education" in Greek, Latin and mathematics. A typical teacher earned $25 a month and a school term lasted four months. However, beginning in the 1830s, and overwhelmingly in the Piedmont, schools sprang up in rapid succession, extending education beyond the privileged few. The Quakers chartered New Garden Boarding School in 1833, which became Guilford College in 1889. The Baptists established Wake

Palmer's Brigade at the Battle of Bentonville, 1865, from a Harper's Magazine *engraving.*

Forest in 1834, the Presbyterians founded Davidson College in 1838 and the Methodists opened Trinity College, which would later become Duke University, in 1839. In 1851 in Newton, the German Reformed Church established Catawba College and in 1857 the Methodists chartered Louisburg College. Institutions of higher learning for women, too, appeared, again primarily in the Piedmont. Salem Female Academy, chartered in 1802 by the Moravians, would become Salem College and be recognized as one of the best schools for women in the south. Greensboro Female College opened in 1838. In Raleigh, the Episcopal Church founded Saint Mary's School in 1838 and the Presbyterians followed with Peace Female Institution in 1857.

The Civil War interrupted this proliferation of education in the Piedmont, and during the war years North Carolina learned a bitter lesson as half-starved soldiers, dressed in rags, faced the best-armed, best-fed army of modern times. The Raleigh *Observer* said in 1869, "The aspirations of the Southern heart are to be recognized by WORK. Out of Southern soil, out of Southern metal, out of Southern wood, out of Southern fabrics, brought out by intelligence, zeal and activity, must come the scepter of our restored power."

The following traditional story reflected a recognition that the diversified northern economy was superior to the South's colonial class system based entirely on agriculture.

"We buried him near a marble quarry, yet the tiny tombstone over his grave came all the way from Vermont.

"We buried him near a magnificent pine forest, yet the coffin was imported from Cincinnati.

"We buried him in a shirt from Chicago, a coat from New York, a pair of breeches from Philadelphia and a pair of socks from Boston.

"The only things the South contributed to that funeral were the corpse and the hole in the ground."

North Carolina apparently learned well the lesson that basing its economy and way of life on the single institution of agriculture led to a dangerous level of dependence. Now the Piedmont, known as the "Dixie Dynamo," celebrates diversification. Charlotte, the largest city in the Carolinas, built its metropolitan-area population of 1.1 million as a business center and a convention city. Its trucking ranks second in the Southeast, and its airport third as a distribution center. Charlotte, the sixth-largest banking center in the United States, has more assets than Atlanta and Miami combined. NCNB, the largest bank in the Southeast, operates from headquarters in the Queen City, as does First Union Bank.

This is a high-energy town works hard and plays hard. The "Mecklenburgers" still exhibit the same spirit that inspired Cornwallis to refer to their village as a "damned hornet's nest," an epithet proudly borne by many local organizations. The new National Basketball Association franchise, the Charlotte Hornets, broke all league attendance records for first-year expansion teams and now leads all NBA teams in attendance. The new Charlotte Coliseum, where the Hornets play home games, is the largest of any NBA team.

Builders of the Mint Museum, North Carolina's first art museum, used materials from the first regional U.S. Mint. Charlotte's mint served the gold-producing southern Appalachian region, the only gold mining region in the country in early colonial times. During the Civil War, the U.S. Mint in Charlotte functioned as a Confederate headquarters and hospital. When the government ordered its destruction in 1932, patriotic Mecklenburgers bought the materials and reconstructed the mint on a site donated by B.C. Griffith.

The Mint Museum, the finest cultural facility in the region, features American and European canvases, African art and historic Piedmont artifacts. The Mint's Dalhem Gallery owns one of

Charlotte's "Mecklenburgers" live in the largest city of the Carolinas—one that works hard and plays hard.

Energetic Charlotte's downtown.

America's premier collections of pottery and porcelain, more than 2,000 pieces from ancient Chinese dynasties to English Wedgwood. The Dalton Collection includes works by Winslow Homer, Thomas Eakins, Andrew Wyeth, Frederic Remington and others.

The Charlotte Symphony, one of the finest in the country, offers performances ranging from formal concerts to the Summer Pops Outdoor Series under the Freedom Park band shell. Charlotte's opera takes the stage in the $35 million Performing Arts Center. The $9.8-million Discovery Place, one of the top 10 science museums in the country, attracts more than 300,000 visitors annually. Discovery Place features a wave tank, a ripple tank, graphic panels on "Our Changing Coast" and a computer game called "Shore Wars." As one of America's best hands-on science and technology museums, Discovery Place offers everything from information on elementary hieroglyphics and mummification techniques to introductory skeleton-assembling classes for young people.

Greensboro is home to the textile giants Burlington Industries, Cone Mills and Wrangler Corporation. Greensboro's Richardson-Vicks U.S.A. leads in health care products. Jefferson Standard, Pilot Life and Southern Life Insurance companies have made Greensboro the "Hartford of the South" as an insurance center.

North Carolina supports 11 black colleges and universities, primarily in the Piedmont, more than any other state in the U.S.

71

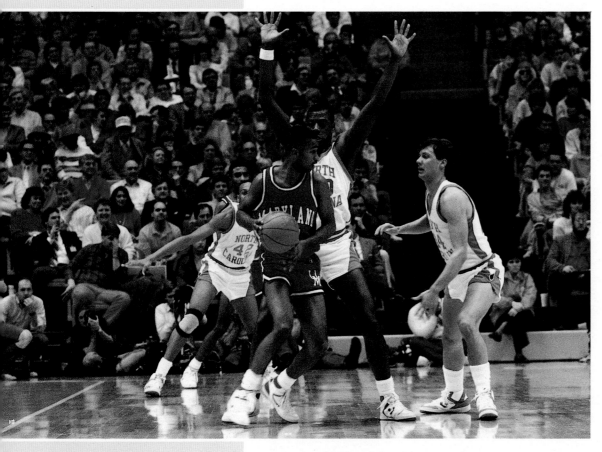

Above: *University of North Carolina, Chapel Hill, in action against Atlantic Coast conference rival Maryland.*

Facing page: *The World 600 stock car race at Charlotte.*

Within the state-wide, 16-member UNC system, only three branches grant Ph.D.s throughout the general curriculum: UNC-Chapel Hill, N.C. State and UNC-Greensboro. UNC-G's men's soccer team has won five of the last six national championships.

The Greensboro Historical Museum, named in *Southern Living* on two different occasions as one of the finest small museums in the country, owns the largest existing display of material on short story writer William Sydney Porter, "O. Henry," who was born and raised in Greensboro. Greensboro's Eastern Music Festival, an internationally acclaimed summer festival offers music from Brahms, Beethoven and Mozart to world premieres by American composers. Its six-week classical concert series features the Eastern Philharmonic Orchestra, composed of musicians from major orchestras and leading music schools around the world.

Aside from commerce and education, Greensboro is known for Blandwood Mansion, home of John Motley Morehead, North Carolina governor from 1841 to 1845, who is credited with unifying the state with a comprehensive transportation system. Governor Morehead's greatest contribution was his leadership in establishing the North Carolina Railroad, which served to dissolve the persistent sectionalism problem. Blandwood is known as one of the first Italianate villas in the U.S. and was one of the most stylish estates in Piedmont North Carolina in the 19th century. Blandwood was designed by Alexander Jackson Davis, one of the most influential architects of the 19th century. It is open to public visitation.

One of the most interesting facilities in Greensboro, the nonprofit Center for Creative Leadership, was founded by the patriarch of the Vicks Chemical Company, H. Smith Richardson Sr. in 1970. The Center goal develops leadership qualities in five categories: Executive Leadership, Innovation and Creativity, Leadership Development, Leadership Technologies, and Education and Nonprofit Sector. The Greensboro-based center operates branches in Colorado Springs, Colorado and San Diego, California. Its teachers present workshops on leadership and creativity to governments and companies all over the world.

Nearby High Point proclaims itself the furniture and hosiery capital of the world. Its Southern Furniture Market, the largest furniture trade show in the world, swells High Point's population by 50,000 twice a year as manufacturers and retailers from around the world convene. High Point hosts the North Carolina Shakespeare Festival, which features national and international talent, and the local repertory theater is now known as one of the finest theater companies in the Southeast.

Greensboro's North Carolina Agricultural and Technical University, part of the University of North Carolina system, the "flagship" of the state's institutions of higher learning for blacks, has implemented programs for leadership development, engineering and agriculture in Africa and the Caribbean and is preparing other such programs for China. Alumni include Jesse Jackson, astronaut Ron MacNair and Brigadier General Clara Adams-Ender. Five percent of all black engineers in the country graduated from North Carolina A&T. Offering courses in 89 fields of study to 6,100 students, North Carolina A&T specializes in engineering, business and science, and offers graduate programs in 40 fields, including a cooperative doctorate program with N.C. State in Raleigh in engineering.

The University of North Carolina at Greensboro, known as Woman's College before 1963, specializes in education, liberal arts, fine arts, music, environmental sciences and creative writing.

Hanes, the giant underwear, sports wear, sleep wear and hosiery manufacturer, makes Winston-Salem its home, as does the prominent regional banking house Wachovia Bank and Trust, ranking 27 nationally in deposits. Winston's R.J. Reynolds has led in production of tobacco since 1872. Whitaker Park, one of the world's most modern cigarette manufacturing centers, can produce 8,000 cigarettes a minute. Stroh's Brewery, one of the world's largest brewing facilities, offers tours that explain every step of beer brewing and packaging.

Winston-Salem boasts both Wake Forest University and its prestigious Bowman Gray School of Medicine–Baptist Hospital, one of four medical schools within the state. The city actively supports the arts and claims the nation's first arts council. Winston's North Carolina School of the Arts, the only state-supported residential school of its kind in the United States, combines schools of dance, design and production, drama and music. Students may work toward a high school diploma with arts concentration, an arts diploma at the college level, or a Bachelor of Fine Arts, Bachelor of Music or Master of Fine Arts degree. Half the student body comes from North Carolina, the rest from around the U.S. and abroad.

Winston-Salem's Southeast Center for Contemporary Art, a unique exhibition and performing center, features the works of the best visual artists of the region and performing artists of national and international reputation. Located in a renovated English country home on 32 acres of rambling woodlands, the center mounts new exhibits every eight weeks.

The Sawtooth Center, a renovated mill, once belonged to the Hanes Knitting Mill. Here some of the area's best-known artists conduct more than 200 workshops and classes serving more than 4,000 participants a year. The three galleries of the Sawtooth building feature traveling exhibits, juried shows and exhibits from area artists.

The Museum of Early Southern Decorative Arts is the only museum in the nation dedicated to exhibiting and researching the regional decorative arts of the South before 1820. The collection includes furniture, paintings, textiles, ceramics and silver and metal ware from Maryland, Virginia, the Carolinas, Georgia, Kentucky and Tennessee. Reynolda House, on the National Register of Historic Places, built by Richard Joshua Reynolds, houses a superb collection of pottery, Tiffany glass displayed in Chippendale corner cabinets, and a fine collection of American art from 1755 to the present.

Old Salem faithfully restores a Moravian community from the late 1700s. Here craftsmen wearing period clothing spin fiber

on authentic spinning wheels, bake bread in wood-fired ovens, mold clay pipes and make shoes. Bethabara Park, the first Moravian settlement in North Carolina, resembles Old Salem on a smaller scale. Winston's Tanglewood features one of the top 10 public PGA golf courses in the U.S., a competition BMX bicycle track, tennis and even polo matches during the spring and fall "Sport of Kings" celebrations.

The "Triad" of Greensboro, High Point and Winston-Salem has attracted numerous large corporations, including American Express (which located a $50 million regional service center in Greensboro) and Konica Manufacturing U.S.A. (which opened a $120 million complex between Greensboro and Burlington). Fieldcrest Cannon, Inc. recently moved its rug and carpet headquarters here from Greenville, South Carolina. Sears Roebuck chose the Triad for its East Coast warranty repair center as did Volvo GM Heavy Truck Corporation, one of the three largest heavy truck manufacturers in the United States. Hyundai Furniture Industries, whose parent company produces the low-priced auto, relocated its corporate headquarters from Dallas to High Point. Honda Power Equipment Manufacturing, Inc. opened a plant in Alamance County to manufacture self-propelled lawn mowers, investing $50 million. In Greensboro, three new office towers—the 18-story United Guaranty Plaza, 19-story Union Tower and 20-story Jefferson-Pilot Tower—represent a combined investment of $85 million. Other new developments include Piedmont Centre, a 1,000-acre mixed-use retail, office, residential and warehouse center, Deep River Corporate Park, Northridge Business Park and Riverbend Industrial Park.

Other corporate giants have occupied the Triad for many years: AT&T, Lorillard, Thomas Bilt (the nation's largest producer of school buses) and Hatteras Yachts (the world's largest builder of pleasure boats). Klaussner Furniture, Eveready Battery, American Tobacco, Glen Raven Mills, Miller Brewery Co., Integon Corporation and Jefferson Pilot also boost the region's economy significantly.

The Raleigh-Durham-Chapel Hill Research Triangle has attracted even more world attention than the Triad. Durham, "City of Medicine," boasts the first downtown district in the state to be placed on the National Register of Historic Places. Duke University ranks as one of the nation's outstanding institutions of higher learning, and Duke Medical Center ranks among the top five medical centers in the nation. The Medical Center operates the world's most advanced hyperbaric center, used in deep-diving studies and for some medical applications. Duke, with only 9,500 students and 1,400 faculty, ranks seventh in the

Left: In Greensboro, a statue of Nathaniel Green, who commanded American forces at the decisive Battle of Guilford Courthouse in the American Revolution. The city is named for him.

Facing page: The Burroughs-Wellcome headquarters in Research Triangle Park.

U.S. among major research institutions and its business school is in the nation's top 10. Duke's interdisciplinary studies include the biomedical engineering department, the institute of statistics and decision science, and the comprehensive cancer research center. The university operates a primate center with the largest collection of prosimians in the world. Duke's library ranks seventh largest among U.S. private colleges. On the East Campus, the Duke University Museum of Art features classical and contemporary American and European medieval sculpture and changing exhibitions of pre-Columbian art and African sculpture. The Duke West Campus is noted for its magnificent Gothic architecture, a 210-foot bell tower patterned after Canterbury Cathedral in England and the $500,000 Flentrop Organ, one of the finest in the Western hemisphere. The 55-acre Sarah P. Duke Gardens here draws about 200,000 visitors annually.

Above: *Re-enactment of the Civil War's Battle of Bentonville.*

Facing page: *The Gothic architecture of Duke University.*

Durham's Stagville Preservation Center is the nation's first state-owned research center for the study of historic and archaeological preservation technology. On Durham's Bennett Place, Confederate General Joseph Johnston surrendered to Union General William Sherman. The 78-acre North Carolina Museum of Science and Life features one of the finest aerospace collections in the Southeast and Durham's North Carolina School of Science and Mathematics is the nation's first residential public high school for students gifted in science and math. West Point on the Eno, in the 400-acre Eno River City Park, offers visitors a working grist mill and blacksmith shop, and the Hugh Mangum Museum of Photography. North Carolina Central University, the nation's first state-supported liberal arts college for blacks, and North Carolina Mutual Life Insurance Company, the largest black-managed financial institution in America, both call Durham home.

The University of North Carolina at Chapel Hill, only 20 minutes from the Duke campus, ranks with the University of Virginia and the University of California as one of the top three public universities in the country. Among major research universities issuing doctorate degrees, Chapel Hill ranks first in the Southeast and 11th nationally, according to the National Academy Press. It is also 11th nationally among business schools, first nationally among schools of dentistry, and among the top 10 in journalism schools. The National Academy of Sciences ranked Chapel Hill's faculty best in the Southeast and the Sociology Department as fourth in the U.S.

Chapel Hill's beautiful campus architecture befits the oldest state university in the country. Old East dormitory, the oldest state university building in the nation, opened while George Washington served his first term as President. Chapel Hill's library ranks among the nation's top 20 research university libraries and the North Carolina Collection of more than 250,000 books, periodicals and other materials—including an outstanding collection of manuscripts by Chapel Hill alumnus Thomas Wolfe—comprise the largest state collection under one roof.

Thomas Wolfe arrived on the campus of the University at the age of 15 in 1916, and described it in *Look Homeward, Angel:* "There was still a good flavor of the wilderness about the place— one felt its remoteness, its isolated charm. It seemed to Eugene like a provincial outpost of great Rome: the wilderness crept up to it like a beast.

"The great poverty, its century-long struggle in the forest, had given the university a sweetness and a beauty it would later forfeit. It had the fine authority of provincialism—the provincialism of an older South. Nothing mattered but the State; the State was a mighty empire, a rich kingdom—there was, beyond, a remote and semi-barbaric world."

Chapel Hill's North Carolina Botanical Garden, a 306-acre woodland, nourishes the largest collection of native plants and herbs in the Southeast. Morehead Planetarium, one of the most sophisticated planetariums in the world and the first of its type located on a university campus in the U.S., has attracted more than 3 million visitors since it opened in 1949.

A remarkable number of historical markers stand along the narrow, shaded streets of nearby Hillsborough. Here Cornwallis flew the Union Jack in an effort to raise conscripts for the British army during the Revolution. In 1788, at the Constitutional Convention in Hillsborough, speakers argued passionately over ratification of the Constitution, since they felt it did not protect the rights of the individual. The North Carolina convention failed to ratify for this reason.

More than 50 structures from the 1700s still stand in Hillsborough. The William Hooper house is one of the few

(continued on page 82)

Research Triangle Park

One of the great success stories in North Carolina's history, Research Triangle Park, has united three great universities and combined a pool of resources with few equals in the world. The Research Triangle is bounded by Duke University in Durham, North Carolina State University in Raleigh, and the University of North Carolina in Chapel Hill. More than 35 separate research facilities representing government, industry and university occupy the largest planned research center in the world. The foundation upon which the center is built is the three universities, which provide a combined enrollment of 60,000 undergraduate students, 11,000 graduate students, and 8 million library volumes with "computer available" and interconnected catalogs. The faculty members of the three universities and the 30,000 scientists, researchers and others employed by Research Triangle, all live and work as part of a unique, synergistic environment.

Research Triangle began in the imaginations of two men, each with a different vision. Dr. Howard Odom, founder in 1924 of the Institute for Research in Social Science at UNC-Chapel Hill, envisioned an academic center for research in social sciences and human relations. In 1952, Dr. Odom wrote three proposals for establishing research institutes to consolidate the activities of branches of the UNC system. His proposals, though unsuccessful, influeenced Dr. George L. Simpson, who became a major player in the formation of the Research Triangle.

At the same time, Romeo Guest, president of Romeo Guest Associates, a Greensboro building firm, was compiling a similar proposal, one that emphasized industrial development. Guest, a graduate of Massachusetts Institute of Technology, had spent time in the Boston area, where he had been impressed with the industrial and research complex on the Charles River. In 1953 he coined the term "Research Triangle." In 1955, Guest presented the idea to Governor Luther Hodges, who appointed the Research Triangle Committee, with former Wachovia Bank and Trust Company president Robert M. Hanes of Winston-Salem as its chairman and Dr. George L. Simpson, Jr. its executive director. Dr. Simpson still believed in the emphasis of his mentor, Dr. Odom, on research. In 1957, The Pinelands Company, with Romeo Guest as president, incorporated as a for-profit company in order to acquire property. However, an economic downturn in 1957 discouraged sales of Pinelands' stock and prospects for Research Triangle Park dimmed.

In 1958, Gov. Hodges asked state senator Archie K. Davis to revive the stalled Research Triangle Park. From 1959 to 1965 the Research Triangle idea caught on so slowly that the Research Triangle Foundation took on a $1.3 million mortgage. Sen. Davis, however, made two suggestions that saved the Research Triangle Park idea. He recommended that the Research Triangle Committee be re-chartered as a not-for-profit corporation and that the foundation acquire ownership of the Pinelands Company and use profits from land sales to support development and promotion of the park.

In May of 1959 the Chemstrand Corporation, a leader in the chemical fiber industry (now called Monsanto Triangle), bought the first tract of land in the park and built a research facility. The park grew slowly until 1965, when IBM announced plans to build a $15 million research, development and manufacturing complex on a 400-acre site within the park. This commitment by a corporate "blue chipper" marked perhaps the most important milestone in the park's history, for by winning the confidence of IBM, the Research Triangle Park

gained credibility with corporate and research communities.

In the 1980s, Research Triangle Park facilities span social and economic systems, human resources, statistical sciences, survey research, chemistry and life sciences, energy engineering and environmental sciences.

Burroughs Wellcome Company, one of the world's foremost pharmaceutical researching and manufacturing companies, transferred all its operations from Tuckahoe, New York to North Carolina in 1970, locating its corporate headquarters in the park and its manufacturing plant in Greenville. The American Association of Textile Chemists and Colorists, the largest textile membership society in the world, maintains its headquarters in the park. IBM's presence has grown into one of the corporation's major facilities world-wide. Northern Telecom, the only manufacturer in the U.S. producing a complete line of digital switching systems, moved into the park in 1981.

The National Center for Health Statistics, affiliated with the U.S. Public Health Service, moved into Research Triangle

CHIP HENDERSON PHOTOS BOTH PAGES

Park in 1966. The Environmental Research Center, the largest field installation of the U.S. Environmental Protection Agency, dedicated its research and development building in 1971. At list of other occupants reads like a who's who of the world's top corporations and includes Troxler Electronic Lab-

oratories, the Chemical Industry Institute of Toxicology, Family Health International, the National Humanities Center, Union Carbide, Compuchem Laboratories Incorporated, General Electric, DuPont, Ciba-Geigy, Sumitomo Electric.

Raleigh-Durham Airport serves the Research Triangle with

seven major and six commuter airlines.

The Research Triangle represents a remarkable achievement with few parallels in the world, bequeathed by the Piedmont's small farmers and craftsmen with their belief in eduction and the value of individual endeavor.

Research Triangle Park attracts some of the best scientific minds in the world.

The Colonial in Hillsborough, one of the oldest continually-operating inns in America.

remaining homes of a signer of the Declaration of Independence. According to local legend, Hillsborough's Colonial Inn, one of the oldest continually-operating inns in the nation, escaped pillaging by the Union forces during the Civil War because a Masonic emblem hung from one of the second-story balconies as Sherman's troops marched through town. The historic inn serves delicious meals in a colonial atmosphere.

Raleigh, the state's capital, has been designated as one of the top medium-sized cities in the U.S. for quality of life by Rand McNally. Government and education are its major employers, and art flourishes. Because of nearby Research Triangle, the Triangle area of Raleigh, Durham and Chapel Hill contains more Ph.D.s per capita than any other area in the U.S. The Triangle cities work together, as they did in the U.S. Olympic Festival of 1988 where all three triangle cities shared sports events equally. Raleigh is an amateur sports mecca and an education center. North Carolina State University, in Raleigh, built the first nuclear reactor on a university campus. The university's one-megawatt PULSTAR educates nuclear engineers, facilitates atomic energy research and provides radiation services for government and industry. State's "phytotron," one of only six in the world, contains more than 50 individually-controlled environmental chambers for plant research, simulating conditions ranging from jungle to arctic tundra.

In addition to 17,000-student North Carolina State, Raleigh is home to Shaw University, Saint Augustine's College, Peace College, Saint Mary's College and Meredith College. Perhaps that is why Raleigh, with a city population of 218,000 and a metropolitan area population of 655,000, supports an unbelievable 194 arts organizations. In addition to the Museum of National History, one of the state's most popular museums, and the North Carolina Museum of History, Raleigh has the North Carolina Museum of Art, the first state museum of art, recognized as possessing the finest collection of art in the Southeast. The Kress Collection of Renaissance and Baroque Art is second in size only to that of the National Gallery of Art in Washington, D.C. The North Carolina Symphony, the first state-supported symphony in the country in 1946, gives more than 200 concerts a season.

Raleigh is a town known to be friendly and relaxed and seems doggedly determined to keep those qualities. It sits only two and a half hours from the Wilmington beaches, halfway between the beaches and the mountains, and is historically tied to the slow-paced graciousness of the vast, agricultural Coastal Plain that stretches eastward just beyond the city limits. Raleigh is fighting urban sprawl by revitalizing the downtown district.

A few miles beyond the city limits of the Piedmont's burgeoning population centers, one slips comfortably back into the easy and the earthy. Just south of Greensboro, around the community of Seagrove, approximately 25 pottery shops exist within a 10-mile radius. The earliest potters here were farmers who "turned" only when farming slowed down long enough for them to throw a few crocks, churns and pickle jars. "Waggoners" moved slowly through the Carolinas and Virginia on dirt tracks and plank roads, selling these simple vessels for five to 15 cents apiece, or bartering them for nails, horseshoes and other items. Large jugs became gravestones.

During the Civil War potters came to the Seagrove area in droves, exempt from serving in the Confederate Army because Robert E. Lee's army desparately needed their crocks, jars and "dirt dishes." "Little brown jugs" became wildly popular at the end of the 19th century. But in 1908 the adoption of Prohibition stopped many potters' wheels and the craft that had flourished since the 1750s in North Carolina's Piedmont suddenly faced oblivion. Where 50 kilns had filled distillers' orders for jugs, after 1908 only a handful survived by producing pitchers, stew pots and sorghum jugs for area residents. Sons of potters left Moore and Randolph counties to work in sawmills, cotton and furniture factories. With the death of each potter, a family's knowledge and technique disappeared, and North Carolina's oldest folk art gave way to cheap, mass-produced "five-and-dime store" pottery.

In 1915, Juliana Royster Busbee, while judging a Davidson County Fair in nearby Lexington, saw a brilliant-orange-glazed pie plate. She became infatuated with it. Mrs. Busbee bought all the pieces with the striking glaze that she could find in Lexington: burnt orange, "tobacco-spit brown" and "frog-skin green."

She showed them to her husband Jacques, a highly trained portrait painter, and the couple vowed to preserve these nearly magical glazes.

The Busbees located Ben Owen, the son of the potter who had made the orange plate, and helped him to master the dying art. Under Mr. Busbee's supervision Ben Owen toured museums in Washington, D.C. and New York, studying the shapes of pieces thrown in China during the Han and Sung dynasties. He became a master potter. Years later Peking experts stated that Ben Owens, from Moore County, North Carolina, had captured, almost to perfection, the subtlety of the Chinese forms. This art form now flourishes in North Carolina's Piedmont like good conversation.

Still under construction in Asheboro, only a few miles from Seagrove, the North Carolina Zoo, will cover the largest land area of any zoo and is the first zoo planned entirely around the natural-habitat concept. The zoo will recreate the seven continents and include a World of Seas. Already visitors to the Africa section can see, without looking through a single set of bars, giraffes, zebras, ostriches, Hamadryads baboons, chimpanzees, Southern white rhinos, African elephants, blue-faced mandrils, gazelles, impala, kudus, secretary birds, marabou

CHIP HENDERSON

storks and Ramar, the lowland gorilla. These animals all live in habitats similar to their natural ones, separated from visitors only by rocks, gullies, moats, vegetation or glass. The zoo participates in "Project Chimpanzoo," Dr. Jane Goodall's study comparing the behavior of wild chimps to captive ones.

About 30 miles west of Asheboro, a 57-acre historic site in Spencer draws steam locomotive fanciers by the thousands each year. Here, in what was the Southern Railway's Master Mechanic office from 1907 until 1960, 2,500 men could service as many as 100 steam locomotives a day. Diesel locomotives closed the Spencer steam shops, but visitors still can see two restored steam locomotives and the "rolling palaces" of a bygone era.

In Gastonia, the Schiele Museum of Natural History and Planetarium owns perhaps the best collection of taxidermied

Friendly and relaxed Raleigh sits halfway between the beaches and the mountains.

The Old Well at University of North Carolina, Chapel Hill.

81

land mammals in the Southeast. The collection ranges from a reconstructed mastodon to a saber-toothed tiger, the only one in the world. Among the museum's 10,000 items are mammals, birds, fish, insects, rocks and minerals, fossils and plants. The museum originated with the personal collection of Bud Schiele, who came to Gastonia to direct the Piedmont Boy Scout Camp. Visitors may watch a blacksmith at work, an operating grist mill, molasses being made or authentic Indian dances. Native American pottery-making demonstrations and other activities reflect diverse cultures. The Schiele Museum has programs on wild foods, early American dance, 18th-century clothing, early American paper making, fire making, split-cane basketry and Woodland-style pottery making.

Salisbury has a National Cemetery where 10,000 Union soldiers who did not survive Salisbury's infamous Confederate prison rest for eternity. The town of Waxhaw, a living antique itself with faded signs, consists of more than 25 old brick stores converted into antiques shops. Visitors and antiques collectors from the entire East Coast fill them each week, where owners sell and barter as if the year were 1850.

Clogging and buck dancing originated in North Carolina, Tennessee and the Southern Appalachian region, but nowhere are they more popular than in the Tar Heel State. This "mountain dancing" evolved with bluegrass music in the mountains, but has come down out of the hills and established itself from Raleigh all the way to the Tennessee border. Several groups from the Piedmont and the mountains, including the five-time national-champion Hickory Flats Hoedowners in Denton, are among the best in the Southeast. Clogging and buck dancing, folk art forms still evolving within the borders of the state, require remarkable athletic ability and stamina, and feature their own colorful, esoteric vocabulary. For every run up and down the guitar neck, a dancer might do a chain step, the stomp double and a clog-over-vine. Every rill on the banjo might call for the waterbug step, a scotty, a chuggy buck and fancy double. And every seesaw and squawk of the fiddle might cue a mule-kick, a pitter-patter basic and a maggie. As the bluegrass musicians play old favorites like "Soldiers' Joy," "Down Yonder," "Black Mountain Rag" and "Tennessee Mountain Clog," the dance combines endless, bizarre, spellbinding movements. As the fiddle wails and the banjo tinkles against bright, powerful guitar chords, the uniformed dancers of a top precision group move through patterns with a synchronization and foot speed that pull gasps from the crowd. The colorful, limber figures of man and woman are as light-footed as deer, metal taps in perfect time with the music, each one twisting and flexing like the jointed,

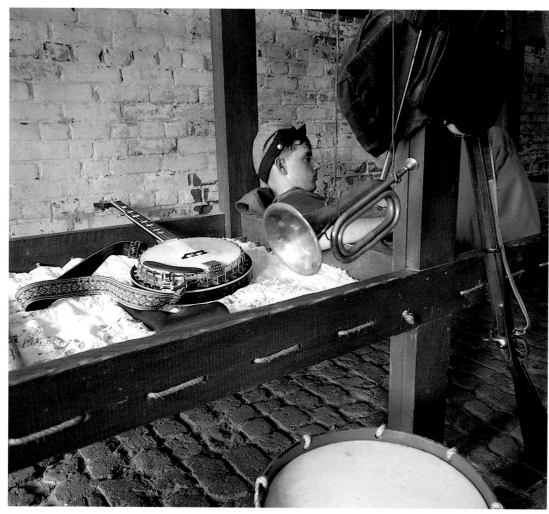

wooden, human-figure toy "limberjack on a string," played on the knee of God.

The Piedmont does not possess vast tracts of unspoiled wilderness as do other regions of the state, but natural recreation lies surprisingly close to population centers. Just north of Hillsborough and Durham, 2,228-acre Eno River State Park has joined federal and local reserves to form a "green belt" 40 miles long, due in large part to the efforts of Margaret Nygard to save the land around the river from development.

West of Sparta flows the oldest river in the Americas, the New. Only the Nile is older in the entire world. The north-flowing New River drew national attention in the mid-1970s when Appalachian Power Company attempted to build two dams on the river near Sparta. Jed Farrington of Jefferson told me about the grassroots movement that began locally and culminated in Washington, spearheaded at the end by Senator Sam Ervin. He spoke with pride of how the locals became passionate about saving the river from becoming just another reservoir, and succeeded in obtaining Wild and Scenic River status for $26\frac{1}{2}$ miles of the New.

South of Greensboro, the Uwharrie National Forest covers 50,000 acres of hardwood forest in Montgomery, Randolph and

Above: *Playing a limberjack at the Aberdeen Farm Festival.*
Left: *A tired graycoat at a Civil War re-enactment.*

Facing page: *A Confederate memorial in Raleigh.*

Above: *North Carolina Capitol, Raleigh.*

Facing page: *Rock climbers on the face of Stone Mountain, in the foothills of the Piedmont.*

Just north of Winston-Salem, 6,000-acre Hanging Rock State Park, within the Sauratown Mountains, offers 17 miles of trails and draws more than 250,000 visitors a year. Pilot Mountain State Park, 20 miles southwest of Hanging Rock, offers 2,152 acres for nearby Greensboro and Winston-Salem residents. Indians and Daniel Boone, too, used the distinctive knob on top of the mountain as a landmark.

Daniel Boone spent 21 years in North Carolina, longer than he did in any other state. Boone was one of a handful of "Long Hunters," frontiersmen from North Carolina, Virginia and Pennsylvania who crossed the mountains into Tennessee and Kentucky on hunting trips that frequently lasted a year or more. Shawnee and Cherokee captured Boone three times, and he lost two sons in Indian attacks. He lived in North Carolina near the present location of Wilkesboro before becoming so disgusted with the same corrupt royal sheriffs who incited the Battle of the Regulators that he left North Carolina for good with his family, bound for Kentucky.

At nearby Mount Airy, the world's largest surface granite quarry attracted quarrymen and granite cutters from Scotland, England and Italy in 1889 when Thomas Woodroff and sons purchased it for $5,000. Their descendants still live in the area. Through the same part of the state ran the Great Wagon Road, the most important north-south travel route in all the colonies. Before the arrival of Europeans, the Iroquois had used its path as they traded, hunted and fought wars. The wagon road, now nearly forgotten, played a major role in the life of the southern colonies, for as the German and the Scotch-Irish became disgruntled with the tyranny of the Crown authorities in the northern colonies, they took the Great Wagon Road for Virginia, North Carolina, South Carolina and Tennessee by the tens of thousands. The wagon road, now a sunken, rutted, tree-filled lane, still can be seen in the woods of Stokes and Forsyth counties.

The centerpiece of 12,000-acre Stone Mountain State Park is a 600-foot-high stone monadnock (as high as a 60-story building). Rock hounds come from all over the Southeast to scale the face of Stone Mountain, while hikers from nearby Greensboro and Winston-Salem enjoy trails across acres of solid granite to the summit.

This is the Piedmont, the world of entrepreneur and high finance, as well as a haven for potters, craftsmen and family farms. If only the hard-working, democratic Moravians, Scotch-Irish, English and Germans of the 1700s could see the Triangle, the Triad and the greater Charlotte Metropolitan area!

Davidson counties. These erosion-resistant remnants of the ancient Ocoee Range are the oldest mountains in North America. Although heavily logged by the Forest Service, the Uwharries offer accessible "wilderness" within an hour's drive of Greensboro or Charlotte. The 33-mile-long Uwharrie Trail and other shorter trails wind through alternating patches of cut-over timber and old re-growth punctuated by huge granite boulders. Rattlesnakes and copperheads, plentiful here, deter fewer hikers than does the autumn onslaught of deer hunters.

Today, in the woods of Stokes and Forsyth counties, you still can see traces of the Great Wagon Road that brought thousands of early settlers here.

Fenberg the Potter

There was no one to be seen when I drove into Jerry Fenberg's yard near Asheboro. The workshop, kiln shed and house stood with windows and doors wide open in the 95-degree summer afternoon. Even the beeches and magnolias couldn't deter the heat and humidity. I glanced into the workshop. There were mounds of red clay, unfired pots and lamp bases, but no Fenberg.

From the swimming hole on the creek that formed the southern property line, I heard swimmers, and a short walk through the woods revealed a timeless scene. Fenberg's sons, Moss and Mike, and daughter, Eve, revelled in the creek where it pooled in front of a large granite formation. They invited me to join them and I was sitting on a large, flat rock with only my head and neck out of the water when Fenberg appeared at the edge of the woods. "There you are," he called. "I was firing the kiln." Back in the workshop he immediately seated himself behind the potter's wheel, threw down a cantaloupe-sized mass of red clay, set the stone wheel spinning, and began to draw from it the shape of a dinner plate.

In the 1960st, Jerry and his wife joined the Peace Corps, left the United States to teach for two years in Puerto Rico, then went to Japan to study ceramics under the master potter and national treasure, Shoji Hamada.

Jerry spoke of his time in the Orient. "They have a sense of connectedness, of being watched over by 10,000 years of ancestors. Can you imagine how comforting that would feel? Japanese strangers would walk up to Charlotte and me and say, 'You American— Pioneer!' They would inflate their chests and flex their arm muscles in a caricature of determination. They admire a nation that survives only the the sweat of its brow and the strength of its convictions, with no ties to the ancients. They live in a culture where departed mentors have left road maps through chaos. The Japanese see us as survivors in the face of unimaginable loneliness, not connected to ancestors, not even connected to the yin and yang of the earth, going it alone, the cowboy riding off into the sunset like a knight errant. They admire the indomitable spirit of America more than I can tell you.

"When Charlotte and I and our first-born son, Taro, who was born in Japan, returned to Memphis, we could have gone anywhere and started our little pottery works, but we came here to central North Carolina, where clay has been turned since the 1700s. I went to other places to get a feel for them, but everywhere else a potter was just another hippie. This was still the Sixties, remember? In the Jugtown-Seagrove area, where potters came over 200 years ago for the clay found here, when you tell people you are a potter, they nod in a way that tells you they take you seriously. They've seen vehicles with license plates from every state and from overseas come to Seagrove to lay their money down for our work.

"Charlotte and I immediately liked this place. The people had a quality of 'lumpiness' that we admired. They just seem to lump up, forming extended families, with the grandparents living across the yard in a trailer and in-laws coming over to borrow the Sunday paper from off your lawn before you get up. We had spent time in Cape Cod and various fashionable, 'high-energy' places where people flitted around and tried everything from Zen to macrobiotic foods. We were ready to lump up, set down and stay!"

He slammed a new mass of clay down on the wheel for emphasis, and pounded it. By now there were half a dozen symmetrical yet slightly different clay plates on the shelf that I had watched rise from the amorphous clay, to be cut off at the base with a string knife.

"I'm not going to tell you of the joys of working the four elements, of the wind and fire of the kiln, and the water I throw on the five pounds of earth as it spins on the wheel. Actually, Tupperware makes a lot more sense." He grinned broadly. "Thank goodness people aren't entirely sensible. The mass-produced plastic surfaces are perfection incarnate. Never a botched pot or a wobbly plate to re-throw. Never a headless lamp base when you take it from the kiln."

His shelves were lined with pieces ready to take to his shop, Humble Mill Pottery. There were huge, black-glazed bowls adorned with yellow carp, teacups with

Jerry Fenberg and vessels awaiting the kiln.

hummingbirds, an ashtray with a scarab. "I'll tell you what's unique about what we produce here. It's our use of glazes, but in particular, it's Charlotte's artwork. She has a connection with the forms and colors of birds, flowers and fish that is truly…Japanese.

"We live with the birds and insects here," he said, motioning to the wide windows and shutters. "There's scarcely a day that passes that I don't see a new bug." Fenberg considers air conditioning an extravagance.

We walked into the kiln shed, where we looked through a small window into the orange inferno of the kiln. There, creek bank clay was metamorphosing into china that could endure for centuries. The pieces seem to glow. "Looks good," he said. From a trash can he picked a handful of tooth-like "cones," made of clay, wilted into various postures of defeat. "These become plastic and droop at precise temperatures, telling me when to stop the kiln.

"You see, I have to manipulate and shape with my hands to be happy. When we first came here I worked at the furniture factory in Asheboro, making Kennedy rocking chairs. Every day I did the same thing, running a lathe, producing the same shape. One night when I came home, I was crazy to do something different. I took sand and filled in the cracks between all the bricks in the floor, rubbing it in with my fingers. Not too creative, but I felt so much better. I guess that's why you won't find Tupperware and Rubbermaid at my dinner table. They're not 'reassuring.' I like to see where hands have been. Maybe that's how we Americans 'connect' like the Japanese do, with those who came before. We can see the connection between ourselves and the person who made the piece. He needed to manipulate and the user subconsciously knows this."

We walked outside and stood under one of his shade trees. "This is the 40-year plan that was in my head when we left Japan. You're lookin' at it. I still can't believe that it's here, that I can touch it. You know, there's a flip side to our 'unbearable loneliness' in the United States, to our 'un-connectedness' with 10,000 years of ancestors. Nothing's absolute here. I can do anything I like. I still can't believe I can walk across the yard in the morning, get my hands on a piece of fine-grained clay, and make something beautiful, then fire it and turn it over to Charlotte with her paints, then glaze it and fire it again, and make a living, all at the same time. The very thought of my jars holding honey, or my pitchers holding iced tea, or my plates arranged around the tables of families across the state! What a thought! That's my 'connection,' with 10,000 great dinner conversations. How's that for Zen?"

The Blue Ridge

CHIP HENDERSON

Above: *Mountain stream in autumn.*

Facing page: *Quilt making is still often done the old-fashioned way in North Carolina.*

North Carolina's mountains, like a well loved book, have been worn smooth with time and handling. While the spectacular Rockies, jagged and stony, have little soil, the Smokies' rich topsoil reaches the ridge lines. When the Rockies and Himalayas were mere hills, the mountains of the Blue Ridge towered thousands of feet high. Hardwoods here go from feathery, light green in spring to brilliant red and gold in autumn. Springs of utterly pure drinking water delight hikers who ramble the winding ridges and valleys.

The dirt of the region bears the footprints of history, and remnants and relics abound. A memorial stands where the aging Cherokee Tasali and his three sons offered themselves to the muskets of General Winfield Scott's men for execution in retribution for the deaths of several soldiers during the round-up of the Cherokee Nation for the Trail of Tears march to Oklahoma. Near Roan Mountain, the dirt path used by John Sevier and his mountain men in 1780 on the way to the Battle of Kings Mountain, crosses the Appalachian Trail. Along the French Broad River stand the deserted "drover towns" of Barner, Sandy Bottom and Stackhouse, dating back to the time when drovers on foot pushed herds of livestock down from the Newport, Tennessee area. Local farmers turned over their cows, goats and even turkeys on consignment to the drovers for sale in Asheville or Greenville, South Carolina. The predecessors of today's traveling salesmen, "drummers," hawked pots, pans and household wares to the folk who seldom left the mountain coves that their ancestors had claimed.

The vast Southern Appalachian region equals in size the combined area of New York State and New England. The "Southern Highlands" include the four western counties of Maryland; the Blue Ridge, Shenandoah Valley, and Allegheny Ridge counties of Virginia; all of West Virginia; eastern Tennessee; eastern Kentucky; western North Carolina; the four northwest counties of South Carolina, northern Georgia and northeast Alabama. North Carolina boasts the highest peaks of the entire 112,000-square-mile Appalachian range.

The state's mountain region begins with the "foothills," which range in elevation from 1,000 to 2,000 feet above sea level. This area extends from Rutherfordton on the south end, to Mount Airy on the north, and features the rolling hills that end abruptly at the feet of the Blue Ridge Mountains. Two great ranges cross North Carolina in a northeast-to-southwest direction, the Blue Ridge and the Unakas, which form the state's western border. These ranges create an elevated tableland traversed by lesser ranges, ridges and valleys. The "lesser" ranges include the Black, Roan, Yellow, New Found, Pisgah, Balsam, Cowee, Nantahala, Cheoah, Tusquitee, Unicoi, Great Smokies, Iron, Bald and Stone Mountain ranges.

In the Great Smokies, Clingman's Dome rises 6,642 feet above sea level and the Black Mountain range contains Mount Mitchell, tallest peak east of the Mississippi at 6,684 feet. North Carolina's entire mountain region, including the foothills, stretches about 250 miles long and up to 150 miles wide. It contains one fifth of North Carolina's area but only one seventh of its population. One county here averages fewer than 16 people per square mile and five counties average fewer than 50. The entire state averages 97 people per square mile.

The mountain region of North Carolina retains more visible ties to its past than any other part of the state. In fact, in many ways, "progress" and industry never invaded the Blue Ridge region as they did the Piedmont and the Coastal Plain. The pride of the mountain people in their crafts, their music and their way of life originated more with survival than art. In the simple but demanding life of a mountain family, the woman until recently spent an entire day doing wash, which she boiled in a huge iron pot while she poked at the clothes with a "battlin'" stick to loosen grime and dirt. Ironing took another full day, as flatirons heated repeatedly in hot coals. By boiling scraps of fat meat in lye solution and adding hickory ashes, she made liquid lye soap, poured it into earthenware crocks while hot, then cut it into bars after it hardened. She made brooms from broom corn grown on the land. Quilting, an eternal task for the womenfolk, used cloth

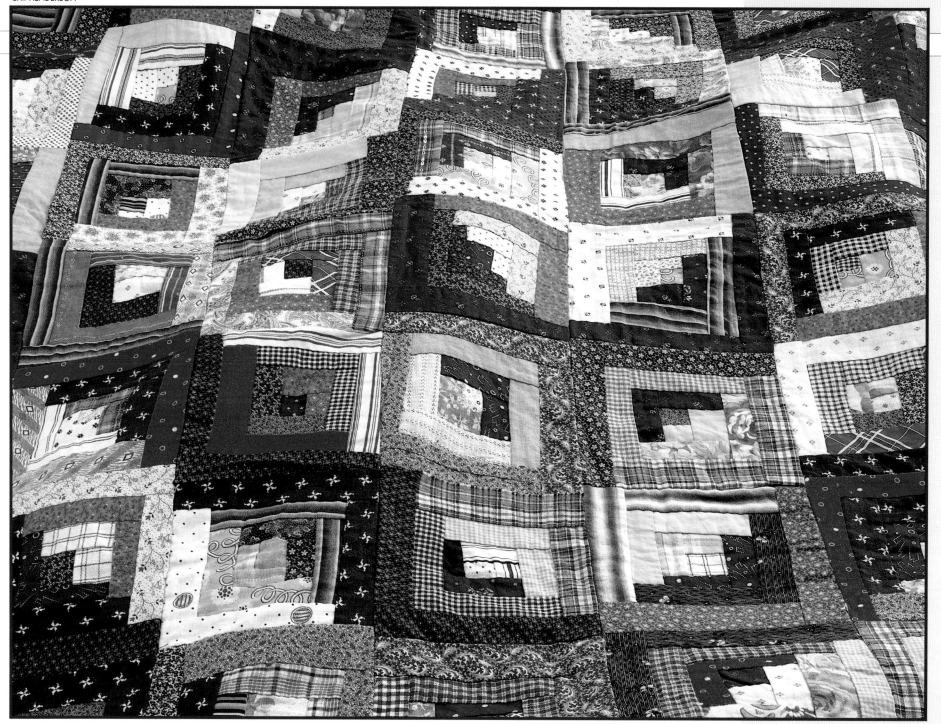

Above: Because of the severe slopes of many cultivated fields in the mountains, there always will be a place for the mule and plow.

Facing page: In mountain homes, more time is spent on the porch than in any other part of the house.

they dyed themselves. Spinning wheels whirred late into the night spinning wool to be dyed in sassafras for a rose-tan color, walnut hulls for brown, sumac for grey, broom sedge for yellow and indigo for blue. Baskets woven from river cane, white oak, hickory and other woods evolved in the Southern Highlands evolved into exactly the same shapes as 4,000-year-old baskets found in Egyptian tombs.

The women administered teas from sassafras, yellow root, wintergreen and wild lady slipper for everything from aches and pains to sleeplessness. One corner of "Mama's" garden was planted in mint, sage, horehound and catnip. "Bornin'" time usually attracted no doctor, and deaths brought all-night vigils in the parlor, with the singing of hymns, whispers and coffee. Mama's *a capella* voice sang lullabies and ballads that her grandparents had sung in Shakespeare's England, to ease the children into sleep.

Papa's "garden" was his Burley tobacco patch. He also planted a patch of buckwheat, for the family loved buckwheat pancakes. He threshed the buckwheat with a hickory flail and winnowed it by pouring it back and forth in canvas until the wind blew away all the chaff. Making sorghum and apple butter were important events, as was a hogkilling. Papa made and repaired the family's shoes and carved utensils such as bread trays, churn dashers and butter paddles from cedar. He bottomed the chairs with hickory splints. All able-bodied men between the ages of 18 and 45 gave three or four days' worth of work each year to maintain the county roads.

In the home, the entire family read and shared a magazine, a Sears catalog, or a letter until it was dog-eared. On long winter evenings children popped corn, roasted chestnuts or cracked walnuts on the hearth. Visiting was a major event and relatives might stay as long as two weeks after the long walk.

In Madison County, a tombstone captured the melancholy of the mountain way of life, the brevity of a human lifetime ever being mocked by the ancient, hazy mountains:

Infant of J. N. and M. L. Rose
Born and Died April 8, 1885
Buded on Earth to Blom in Heaven.

Yet there were times of joy in the mountains. Children carried pails to the berry patches for wild strawberries, dewberries, blackberries and huckleberries that became jelly and jam. Summer revival meetings, after the crops were put up, gave adults the chance to unwind and a boy of courting age could go "sparking" by politely asking the girl of his choice if they could "see her home tonight." Christmas was the happiest of all times. Mountain people exchanged gifts only occasionally, but they found the spirit of Christmas in the smell of a cedar tree, in oranges and apples and peppermint candy and pies baked in a wood stove.

A strong sense of community pervaded the coves and valleys and creeks, where a neighbor delivered a message by "hollerin'." A neighbor's cabin might be a whoop and a holler up the creek, which in linear distance would translate into about a mile. The women reigned supreme in hollerin', since their high-pitched voices could carry up the valley or hollow as light and easy as doves in flight.

The hearty English and Scotch-Irish and German mountain people had to create what they needed with their own imaginations and the materials at hand. They earned little money and obtained most goods by bartering. The mountain people became independent and self-sufficient in heroic proportions.

Appalachian folk-art authority John Campbell has said, "If the question were submitted to an impartial jury as to what is the chief trait of Highland people the world over, the answer would be independence. Should one ask the outstanding trait manifested by the pioneer, the reply would be independence. Inquire what is the characteristic trait of rural folk, particularly of the farming class, and independence will again be the answer. Put the query as to what is the prevailing trait of the American and the unanimous verdict is likely to be independence. We have then, in the Southern Highlander, an American, a rural dweller of the agricultural class, and a mountaineer who is still more or less of a pioneer. His dominant trait is independence raised to the fourth power."

North Carolina's mountain region is not isolated today as before, for highways have connected the remote coves and valleys to the rest of the world. Comfort aplenty now graces the grand inns and resort towns of Blowing Rock, Highlands, Linville and Cashiers. Yet Mama's and Papa's lingering spirits give the North Carolina mountains their identity, and the music and crafts of the region are the tangible legacy of their indomitable character. Basketweavers still ply one of the oldest crafts in the world, some using a little-known double-weave technique. Broom makers tie their home-grown broom corn with poplar rawhide. Cone crafters make wreaths of cones. Cabinetmakers use native black walnut, maple, birch and mahogany. Cornshuck workers make shuck doormats for muddy boots as well as braided shuck collars for mules. Doll makers fill cornshucks with cotton to make plump bodies, use pen and ink to create little faces, make hair from corn silk and hand-sew tiny clothes. Spinners use wool, cotton, flax and yarn. Violin makers craft "fiddles" from North Carolina spruce. Weavers make rugs, coverlets and bags. Woodworkers not only carve, but also create mosaics of inlaid wood that look like paintings. Gunsmiths, wrought iron workers, dulcimer makers, jewelry makers, lapidaries, pewtersmiths, rug makers, silk-screen printers, enamelists, fringers and knotters and block printers still ply their trades.

The Great Smoky Mountains National Park, the largest

(continued on page 97)

Fishing the Dusky Dark

I have a friend who was born and raised in the heart of the Smoky Mountains, along Big Creek, on the Tennessee border. Not long ago we fished together, talking quietly above the soft roar of numerous small cataracts under the newly leafed trees. We started out well in advance of the dusk, to limber our rods, finetune our eyes, and learn the mood of the creek. One of us fished several pools while the other stood to the side and watched the fly ride the tur-

Below: Joe Parkins of Big Creek.

Facing page: Big Creek.

bulent waters, hoping for a rising fish. Joe is left-handed and he remarked to me after half an hour's fishing, "This is a left-handed creek, you know. Have you noticed how much easier it is to backcast to the left?" This was Joe's polite way of giving me an excuse for hanging so many backcasts in the branches overhead, on the right side.

I watched his casts as we moved upstream through several pools. He seldom looked back, yet his backcasts flicked under or above the branches as unerringly as a radar-assisted bat in flight. He memorized branches as we waded up the brook, and only occasionally needed to look back. The sun was just dropping behind the mountains at seven o'clock. The patches of light were still bright on the water. A hummingbird sizzled past our ears, boring through the branches with speed too quick to follow. Joe whispered, "Hummer, lookin' for honeysuckle." Honeybees searched about like tiny, trailing hounds. "Lookin' for pink root," he said. "You've heard of sourwood honey, I bet. Well, I've watched the honey bees for years, never seen one land on a

sourwood blossom. It's the pink root they go for...and the sourwood takes all the credit." He shook his head in deep and tragic sympathy for the lowly pink root.

"Will there be dogs in Heaven?" I asked Joe. He looked quickly at me to see if I was serious, then smiled broadly at the sheer joy of the very thought. We laughed together. My spaniel Jeb retrieved several trout that Joe hooked. He dropped them into my hands without knocking off a single scale. The trout were wild, not hatchery fish, and were as delicately colored as the mountains were secretive. And Joe, the keeper of more secrets than I'll ever know, exhaled long and slow and said, "Well, I'll be—a fish retriever." He got down into a crouch and looked Jeb in the eyes. "Didn't nobody teach you that, did they, boy?"

As we fished up Big Creek, Joe, sensing my eagerness to learn from him, spoke freely. "This little brook's got her moods alright. Turns off and on like a refrigerator. A cloudy day's the best. The magic temperature is somewhere in the mid-sixties, I'd guess. Only the trout know for sure. When the

water rises above it or falls below it, the fish quit feeding. On a normal day the sun warms up the creek to the turn-on point at around nine or ten in the morning. There may be a short hatch of flies, and it stays too warm for anything much to happen for the rest of the day, until it turns on for a little while right at dusky dark. Now, on a cloudy day when the sun peeps out and then goes in and then comes out again, the water temperature keeps changing its mind around 65 degrees. Well, on those days the mayflies rise from the water like an upside-down snow shower. You never dreamed Big Creek could hold so many fish."

I tried to imagine such a sight, thousands of mayflies rising from the dark, tumbling waters into the brief corridor of space above the creek, underneath the arching branches, the fish rising in every pool and riffle.

"You have to put in your days with 'er before she'll show you a sight like that. Once in a while these mountains go a little bit crazy. In 1968 the gray squirrel population was at a high point. The mast crop failed. There wasn't a hickory nut or an acorn to be found. The squirrels migrated from the hills like locusts. I counted thirty dead on the highway in just a few miles. They drowned swimming across Fontana Lake and washed ashore by the thousands. But most of the time it's just like this."

From some distant tree on a ridge above us a rain crow, the local name for the yellow-billed cuckoo, promised a shower, slowly calling "skow, skow, skow," sounding more like the croaking of a tree frog than the call of a bird.

I thought of how different these mountains were from the rest of the state. Here mastery was all in stealth and in timing and in knowing when each mechanism wakes up and turns on for a brief time. I looked at the ferns, flowering plants, shrubs, trees and wild flowers that climbed up and over one ridge after another, a veritable botanical garden. But the secrets are well hidden, being forgotten as the old mountain folk die.

We fished past the public campground at the entrance to the Great Smoky Mountains National Park. As we passed a group of tents the peculiar smell of marijuana smoke wafted down the corridor of the creek. Joe looked at me and a slow, crafty smile spread across his face. "Now can you smell that? Used to be moonshine, but now it's marijuana. Know what some of the old mountain people call it?" he asked me. "The merry widder."

"Perfect," I said.

Joe nodded in agreement. His face quickly turned somber. "Seems like the kids who don't know how to enjoy these hills just naturally get bored and fall in with drugs. But you've got to have a teacher when you're young. That's the time."

And now it was dusky dark and Big Creek turned on and mayflies rose through the gloaming light like tiny souls bound for heaven. Many rode the waters briefly, as their wings dried, and the fish rose to them confidently. We cast our flies among them, or at least Joe did. My first excited cast snarled high in the branches overhanging the right side of the creek. I lost my last light cahill fly. I stood at Joe's side and watched. "Now's the time," he whispered, as his shy mistress let down her hair, as he knew she would.

Bryson City, nestled in the mountains.

JOHN RUCKER

94

CHIP HENDERSON

More than 800 miles of trails wind through the more than 800 square miles of Great Smoky Mountains National Park.

Early fall colors in the Blue Ridge.

wilderness area in the eastern United States, contains more than 800 square miles and more than 800 miles of trails. Congress created what is now the nation's most popular national park in 1926, with about half of it in Tennessee and half in North Carolina

Designated an International Biome Reserve, more than one third of the park supports virgin hardwood and red spruce forests, the largest stand of virgin hardwoods in the United States. Here are the oldest and largest of the eastern hemlock, red spruce, yellow birch, tupelo, yellow buckeye, cucumber magnolia and poplar. Within the park a hiker can traverse climate zones in the

one-day equivalent of walking from Georgia to Canada. For every 1,000 feet of elevation gained, the temperature drops more than two degrees and the vegetation changes as though the hiker had moved 200 miles north. Here, differences in soil moisture, light exposure and slope orientation have resulted in a botanical diversity impossible to match outside the Tropics. The boundaries of the park contain 160 species of trees, more than 1,000 kinds of shrubs, 330 mosses, 1,230 lichens and 600 miles of spring-fed streams. Conditions range from subtropical forests to subarctic peaks.

Once, parts of the park supported thriving human

The Appalachian Trail reaches its highest point at 6,600-ft. Clingman's Dome in North Carolina.

Wolfe's angel—fashioned by W.O. Wolfe of Asheville—inspired the title of son Thomas's novel Look Homeward, Angel.

communities. In the 1850s, Cade's Cove supported 685 residents and 1,200 lived in the Cataloochee area. In 1925, yearly income of families living in what is now the park averaged $125 per year. Now the only permanent residents are black bear, deer, fox, wild boar and wild brook trout.

The park offers delights on many levels. The Oconaluftee Pioneer Farmstead preserves a typical mountain farm and provides demonstrations of early farming methods. The park offers seven developed campgrounds to accommodate recreational vehicles and three primitive campgrounds providing only water and tent sites. Dozens of privately owned campgrounds surround the park.

Primarily catch-and-release fishing within the park features wild brook trout. Hikers can find any challenge they desire in the park, from day hikes to Andrews Bald, Chasteen Creek, Flat Creek Bald, Mingus Creek, Mount Sterling and others, to true back-country hikes. One hundred back-country hiking campsites, located throughout the park, individually accommodate from eight to 20 people for up to three days, but require reservations. Camping outside designated sites is not permitted.

The Appalachian Trail runs 70 miles along the North Carolina-Tennessee border on the highest ridges of the Great Smoky Mountains National Park. Two sections of the trail invite day hikes, both originating in the parking lot at Newfound Gap. To reach Charlie's Bunion and a spectacular view, hike east four miles to a sheer drop of 1,000 feet. To reach Clingman's Dome, follow the trail west for seven and a half miles to reach the highest point on the entire Appalachian Trail at 6,600 feet.

The Appalachian Trail, the world's longest continuous footpath, winds through North Carolina's most splendid mountain regions, covering more than 2,000 miles from Springer Mountain, Georgia to Mt. Katahdin, Maine. Workers cleared the first sections of the trail in 1922 in New York State. The Appalachian Trail traverses rural eastern America, including not only the virgin forests of the Smokies but also the cow pastures of Pennsylvania and the abandoned stagecoach roads of Connecticut. Day users compile most of the trail's user-hours. Long-distance hikers constitute only a small fraction of users and Maine-to-Georgia hikers are few indeed. Since the first "end-to-ender," fewer than 300 people have completed the trail entirely in one year. Yet the trail was conceived for the long-distance hiker.

Asheville, the Queen of the Appalachians, is cradled in the very bosom of the Appalachian mountain chain. Asheville sits at 2,216 feet above sea level on a high plateau surrounded by the Blue Ridge, Pisgah and Newfound mountain ranges. The city's population, having come from all parts of the country to live in the mountains, seems cosmopolitan rather than typically southern. Forty miles from the eastern entrance of the Great Smoky Mountains National Park, the city is in the middle of recreational areas totaling more than a million acres.

As late as 1824, the Asheville area constituted little more than a "stage stop" between the two Greenvilles (South Carolina and Tennessee). During the early colonial era, no settlements occupied the area because the British had guaranteed the territorial integrity of the Cherokee by fixing the boundary of white domain at the foot of the Blue Ridge Mountains.

After construction of the Buncombe Turnpike in 1824, the region began to attract health seekers and those eager to escape the summer heat. Prominent doctors in the East began recommending Asheville to patients with tuberculosis or any illness that demanded rest and fresh air. When the railroad arrived in 1880, those seeking health came in even greater numbers and boarding houses sprang up. Julia Wolfe ran one of these and her son Thomas called it "the Dixieland" when he wrote of the boarders in *Look Homeward, Angel*.

The 1929 crash of the stock market ruined many who speculated on Asheville's real estate, and medical advances eliminated the need for mountain air to treat tuberculosis. Asheville slipped into lethargy for a time, but now a new

generation seeking quality of life has re-discovered Asheville. Tourism is at an all-time high.

One of Asheville's main attractions, the Biltmore House, recalls the era of American history when ruthless businessmen amassed great fortunes, often at the expense of the environment. Cornelius Vanderbilt from New York was such a man. He died before environmentalism or inheritance taxes and left a fortune

Grove Park Inn, Asheville.

Biltmore House—the grandest private residence in the world.

The most imposing hotel in Asheville is the turn-of-the-century Grove Park Inn, built from native stone set in place in such a way as to highlight the natural, weathered surfaces of granite. The bedroom furniture was made by one of the early North Carolina furniture companies, White Furniture of Mebane, which helped make the Piedmont region the world leader in furniture. All the inn's rugs were woven in Aubusson, France and all bedspreads and linen were linen imported from Ireland. Thomas Edison, Henry Ford, John D. Rockefeller, Presidents Wilson, Taft, Coolidge, Hoover, Franklin Roosevelt, Eisenhower, as well as the Mayo brothers, stayed in the inn. Grove Park Inn was enrolled in the National Register of Historic Places in 1973.

Any admirer of the fiction of Thomas Wolfe should visit the setting for his 1934 novel, *Look Homeward, Angel*, the "Old Kentucky Home" run by Wolfe's mother, Julia. The boarding house preserved on Spruce Street in downtown Asheville contains furniture that Wolfe used, as well as personal effects from his New York apartment. The short story writer O. Henry also lived in Asheville and is buried there, as is Wolfe. F. Scott Fitzgerald lived in Asheville while his wife Zelda was in a nearby mental institution. He spent a great deal of time at the Grove Park Inn.

E.W. Grove, who designed Grove Park Inn, also designed the 1920s Gothic Building in downtown Asheville. The building, sometimes called America's first indoor mall, features spiral staircases, gargoyles and brass railings. The Gothic Building encloses the National Climatic Center and National Weather Records Center, the largest such archive in the world. Records of weather all over the United States are collected, stored and analyzed here. On guided tours, visitors can watch meteorological data being entered into computers and computer-tape archives.

Occupying 10 acres of the campus of U.N.C. at Asheville, the University Botanical Garden, contains a sculpture garden for the blind in addition to 26,000 native plants.

Reflecting a blend of sophistication and earthiness, Asheville supports three performing arts centers, a symphony orchestra—and a weekly outdoor hoedown during summer, the Western North Carolina Farmer's Market, one of the most modern, best-planned markets in the United States. Here 1,600 farmers sell fresh sweet corn, tree-ripened apples, peaches, vine-ripened tomatoes and a multitude of other fruits and vegetables in 138 stalls occupying 36 acres.

The Blue Ridge Parkway runs within a few miles of Asheville and visitors from the entire East Coast pass through continuously as they view the light green spring foliage in June, the autumn colors in September and early October, and even the stark yet

to his grandson George, who traveled throughout Europe. The French chateaux of the Loire River Valley, in particular Chambord and Blois, captivated young Vanderbilt. He arrived in Asheville in 1889, bought 130,000 acres of mountain land and developed Biltmore Estate with its great chateau, the largest private residence in the world. The mansion, with 250 rooms, was begun in 1890 and completed five years later. The Biltmore region became the first large tract of managed forest in the nation and, in 1898, site of the first school of forestry in the United States.

In 1916, Mrs. Vanderbilt sold 80,600 acres to the U.S. Government to form the nucleus of the Pisgah National Forest. Biltmore House, the 8,000 remaining acres of woodland—including a winery and 50 acres of gardens and terraces—remain as a stunning monument to extravagance. Biltmore House is open to the public, but a ticket is expensive.

beautiful hardwood forest in winter. North Carolina's Parkway joins the Skyline Drive in Virginia to wind through essentially unspoiled natural beauty for 575 miles, from the upper end of Shenandoah National Park in northern Virginia to the southern border of Great Smoky Mountains National Park, where the parkway rises to its greatest heights and most breathtaking views. The Blue Ridge Parkway is actually a national park, although a narrow one, averaging only 800 feet wide, but it dissects other national parks for half its length.

In the summer of 1988, I went to hear pianist Alexander Peskanov one afternoon at the Brevard Music Festival, which runs week after week each summer. The audience sat in the modernistic open-air auditorium, which has no walls, only huge wooden supports for a massive domed roof. The mountain air moves freely through the structure, which seats hundreds. As the Brevard Music Center Orchestra followed Peskanov's keyboard pyrotechnics with the crash of cymbals and the thunder of kettledrums, it was as though the musicians' energy had awakened the mountains themselves. Thunder began to roll from the hills as if to answer the percussionists, and lightning flashed in concert with the cymbals. A cold, sweet-smelling wind moved through the forest, then invited itself into the auditorium with a scattering of programs. As we clapped feverishly for both man and nature, a cold, hard rain drummed on the roof—only to stop minutes later, leaving us all in silence, watching mist billow up in the nearby forest.

Penland School of Crafts, the oldest and largest crafts school in the country, opened near Spruce Pine in 1929 to preserve traditional mountain crafts. When Miss Lucy Morgan, a primary schoolteacher at the Appalachian School in Penland, became distressed at the virtual disappearance of the art of handweaving in the mountains, she ordered three lightweight looms through the mail. She began to teach weaving in the homes of local women. Then each neighbor donated a log and a day's labor to build a craft house, where she gave weaving lessons. From this humble beginning, Penland grew into an institution with 47 structures, 470 acres, and more than 150 contributing instructors, each of whom usually teaches one class per year. They come from all over the United States and Europe and offer courses in clay, fiber and surface design, glass, metals, print arts, paper, photography and wood. During the summer sessions, Penland can accommodate 125 students per session, but during the spring and fall sessions the curriculum accommodates fewer students with greater intensity.

The finest crafts teachers and practitioners in the world

teach at Penland, without payment, and have since its inception. Studios remain open 24 hours a day.

However, Penland is a folk school were people already proficient in their craft come to perfect it. The John C. Campbell School in Brasstown is North Carolina's other folk institution, and is for the more casual, even the beginning, dancer or craftsperson. Like Penland, the setting is deep in the mountains.

The week I was there, over a hundred grade school children gathered at wooden tables under a vast shelter and free-spirited instructors encouraged them to paint, to braid and weave, and to work in clay. In a similar screened-in shelter, Don Thompkins taught clog dancing daily from nine until four thirty. At night, parents from all over Clay and Cherokee counties brought their children to Don. He had been to all the grade schools in the area and demonstrated his craft; he offered free instruction to all children who had been moved by his fleet-footed performances.

(continued on page 105)

Asheville exhibits a blend of sophistication and earthiness—from symphony to weekly summer hoedowns.

The outdoor drama "Unto These Hills," the story of the Cheokee Nation, is presented west of Asheville.

Hmong of the Blue Ridge

In the foothills of the Smokies, North Carolinians have "done themselves proud." Their story stretches from the refugee centers of Thailand to the Blue Ridge Mountains.

The Reverend Allen McKinney of Marion was watching television one evening in 1974 when the national news featured the plight of the boat people. A newsclip showed thousands fleeing from the communists after the fall of Vietnam, streaming into Thailand or taking to the South China Sea in tiny boats, risking capture by Vietnamese patrol boats and stormy, shark-infested waters. McKinney decided to help as much as a minister in a small North Carolina town could. He spoke to his congregation that Sunday, saying, "We can curse the darkness, or we can get involved." Soon, church members were phoning the Catholic Refugee Office in Charlotte and other groups involved in the Hmong resettlement effort.

Allen learned that the early Hmong resettlement efforts in the U.S. had failed. Resettlement officials could not consider individual needs of the various groups that flooded into the U.S. after the fall of Vietnam, 850,000 Southeast Asians in all. Among them were the quiet Hmong.

In Laos, the Hmong had lived close to nature, with strong clan and family ties. The Hmong had been friendly and warm, but in their harsh new world, many became suspicious and withdrawn. In California, state welfare inspectors who made unannounced visits to Hmong homes received death threats. The Hmongs' warm, gregarious nature arises from fierce independence. They migrated from China long ago and occupied the mountain tops of Laos, claiming land that the Lowland Laotians never considered worth farming. Living in the notorious Golden Triangle, practicing slash-and-burn agriculture, the Hmong had to be tough and determined to survive. In the Vietnam War, the Hmong, financed by the CIA, formed a secret army that fought the communist forces. They suffered casualties at five times the rate of U.S. servicemen. Nearly all adult Hmong are Vietnam veterans.

While Allen McKinney and his group did move some Hmong directly from the refugee centers in Thailand, where 55,000 still wait along the Mekong River in camps, most of the 600 Hmong who came to the Marion-Morganton area relocated from other U.S. cities, where resettlement efforts were causing problems: the San Jaoquin Valley of California (with 23,000 Hmong living in Fresno alone), Wisconsin, Montana, Pennsylvania, Texas and the Minneapolis-St. Paul area.

The Hmong are as resourceful here in North Carolina as they were in Laos. They buy live chickens, pigs, and beef cattle and slaughter them themselves. Now the Hmong are leasing land from area landowners, and a few have purchased their own land. To a Hmong, land is everything. In the October 1988 issue of *National Geographic Magazine*, Spencer Sherman writes that, in Marion and Morganton, "the newcomers have found a measure of prosperity unmatched by other Hmong immigrant farmers around the United States…Virtually all adults are employed."

Allen and his group followed

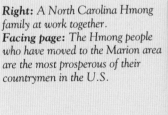

Right: A North Carolina Hmong family at work together.
Facing page: The Hmong people who have moved to the Marion area are the most prosperous of their countrymen in the U.S.

JONA BRADLY

through once the Hmong arrived, finding them jobs and places to live. Ron McRae at the Hmong Naturalization Association said that the Hmong were extremely hard workers. "They didn't have weekends and holidays in the Old Country," he told me. "They never stopped working.

"We've got a good start here, but we have to keep the momentum going. We're setting up monthly meetings with college representatives, business leaders, and Hmong who have been successful. Venture capital is needed. I've talked to some of the California Hmong. I sense that many plan to return to Laos when the political climate changes. Our Hmong are here to stay."

In Morganton I met Kue Chaw, a Hmong leader, and recalled the determination of the Scotch-Irish who had settled in the area 150 years ago. Those Scotch-Irish immigrants claimed the highlands of the Southern Appalachians because the mountains reminded them of their homeland. They, too, were fiercely independent, had strong clan and family ties. Now the Hmong were finding more acceptance in North Caro-

lina than in some other parts of the U.S.

Kue Chaw insisted that I sit at his desk. "So you can write in your notebook," he explained. He seemed delighted to speak to me, eager to explain the Hmong perspective. The first thing he mentioned was how important it was to reestablish the same closeness to nature and the same work ethic his people had known in the Laotian highlands. "Here is much like home, many mountains," he said.

We both looked out the window at the rounded hills. I studied the map and pictures on the wall. The Laotian highlands were, indeed, dead ringers for the Blue Ridge Mountains. He explained that in Laos, "you put a mark on a tree as a boundary and that land is yours if it is not taken." I pointed out to him that North Carolina had nearly four times as many people as Laos.

"There wouldn't be room for everyone to just 'claim' the land they needed."

"Still," he said, "it isn't fair for one man to own ten thousand acres and another man to own nothing."

I nodded. Kue Chaw continued. "And here, all land is claimed, even up to the mountain tops." He was emphatic, for the Hmong had always been able to find idle land for dryland rice farming high in the mountains. "Everywhere are 'walls'," he said, emphasizing his choice of words. "No trespassing.

"And it is wrong for one man to take God's beautiful earth and ruin it to make a lot of money," he said later.

Then Kue Chaw softened and said, "But the best thing of all is freedom. I can tell you exactly what I really think." He smiled broadly. "And here people do this all the time." He made a waving motion. "Nowhere else in U.S. did they do that. And when they say they will help, they keep their word. Here I visit houses. I see pictures on the walls of ancestors standing in the fields. I see old farming machinery standing behind the barn. The people are connected to the land, and their ancestors. Here is the 'bridge' between Hmong and North Carolina people."

I told Kue Chaw of Montana where there was more land, and much of it public. "I was there. I had a relative in Missoula. In Montana they didn't do this to me. He again waved delightedly at me. He said softly, "I think we have found the right place."

That afternoon, I accompanied Kue Chaw to a Hmong funeral. The young woman lying in a casket was about my age. The cause of death was uncertain. Since the Hmong have come to America, 115 have died of Sudden Death Syndrome, and the consensus is that stress is the underlying cause.

As the funeral procession, burning headlights, threaded its way through much of Morganton, the local residents, seeing the Hmong drivers, showed their respect. Traffic stopped and pulled over everywhere the procession went. It was a touching display of empathy by the entire community of Morganton. At the burial site, I thought about Allen McKinney's words, "Our Hmong are here to stay." I tried to think of the separation the dead woman's family must be feeling, to be burying their loved one in this strange new place, this land of giants where freeways filled with cars flow like rivers. Like all epic human relocations, the price was high. The Hmong shed bitter tears as the casket was lowered out of sight. But then I thought again about the North Carolina mountain folk of the foothills. In fact, I realized, as I stood among the Hmong at the grave site, that they have precisely the same traits as Southerners: selflessness, pride, manners, fierce stoicism, fatalism, a deep love for the land.

Retired Elderhostel couples from Wisconsin to New York to Florida Studied lost-wax jewelry technique, wood carving, weaving, blacksmithing and pottery.

Throughout the mountains I heard the hill people use language as I hoped they would, rich with powerful metaphors and proverbial wisdom. I heard one man comment that his neighbor was not inclined to work. Another pondered that, then added, "Lazy…why he wouldn't hit a lick to kill a snake!" I heard stories of highly individualistic dogs that had developed, entirely on their own, the peculiar passion of hunting copperheads and rattlesnakes and "dueling" with them to the death. I heard mountain people refer to the Plott hounds, the oldest American-bred hunting dogs, which the Plott family selectively bred since 1750 west of Waynesville. In 1750, when two Plott brothers, gamekeepers for wealthy landowners, left Germany they brought three brindle and two buckskin hunting dogs. One of the brothers died at sea, but 16-year-old Johannes arrived safely in Philadelphia before following other Germans to North Carolina. The family went on to breed their German hunting dog strain in the redoubtable Plott hound, world-famous for tenacity.

I watched a light plane dart through the mountain passes and buzz the ridges searching for marijuana patches. A generation ago it was revenuers and moonshine distillers, stalking the hills and matching wits. The mountains still provide the backdrop for the timeless dialectic of strong wills.

I heard references to the "Melungeons," a race of olive-skinned, gypsy-like people with dreamy, almost Oriental eyes. Some hill people claim the Melungeons descended from de Soto's Spaniards who came through the region in 1540 searching for gold. Other hill people disagree, arguing that the Melungeons were Portuguese or even Moors who sailed to the New World in their own *Mayflower* and established a colony in North Carolina long before the American Revolution. They had been a carefree, but shy and reticent, people, seldom marrying outside their own. They gradually vanished.

Families speak of ancestral farms and graveyards flooded by the Tennessee Valley Authority lakes. Where Fontana, Hiwassee, Santeetlah and other reservoirs now sparkle, communities once thrived. An old woman in Cullowhee spoke of the cabin where her grandparents homesteaded; in dry years, when the water level drops, she can visit the graveyard where her parents lay. "Come Decoration Day when we mountain folk leave flowers at the graves of our people, I treasure a dry summer when I can get there."

The North Carolina mountains have given so much to the state. Their forests cut down on every mountainside and hauled away to make a handful of ruthless men wealthy, leaving the rest of us poorer. Still, the mountains offer peace and beauty. Yet now a new, more insidious enemy, acid rain, has renewed the attack on the ancient hills. I learned from Jane Sutton, a conservation officer with the Folk Art Center on the Blue Ridge Parkway, that the growth of trees on the high ridges of Mount Mitchell and other high peaks has virtually sopped. Microscopic examination of tree rings reveals practically no measurable growth between yearly growth rings. Acid rain is killing our mountaintop spruce-fir forest, a remnant of the glacial age and unique in all the world. Trees are dying at an alarming rate as 200 pounds of chemicals per acre fall on Mt. Mitchell and other peaks, each year.

Native Americans believe that the trees are relatives of humans. Sometimes they call humans "the walking people," and trees "the standing people." Cherokee/Appalachian poet Marilou Awiakta has written about the dying of both peoples:

Rhododendron on the lower slopes of Mt. Mitchell.

Dying Back

On the mountain
the standing people are dying back—
hemlock, spruce and pine
turn brown in the head.
The hardwood shrivels in new leaf.
Unnatural death
from acid greed
that takes the form of rain
and fog and cloud.

In the valley
the walking people are blank-eyed.
Elders mouth vacant thought.
Youth grow spindly, wan
from sap too drugged to rise.
Pushers drain it off—
sap is gold to them.
The walking people are dying back
as all species do
that kill their own seed.

© *Marilou Awiakta. Originally published in* Parkway Milepost, *Spring/Summer 1988.*

GLENN VAN NIMWEGEN

103

The Old Lady on the Hill

In writing of the mountains, I sought a subject that captured the essence of the Southern Highlands: history, elegance and mystery, all in one, a summation of the character of the region. I considered many subjects, and finally found what I was looking for in the form of an old inn, described in Jerry Bledsoe's column in the Greensboro paper. It was a turn-of-the-century hotel, struggling for survival, known throughout the area as "The Old Lady on the Hill."

My first impression of the "Old Lady on the Hill" was that she had not changed much in 82 years. In spite of needing a new roof and a new coat of paint, it retained an undeniable stateliness. I waited in the lobby for Bob LaBranch, who runs the inn and has been an important figure there for 21 years. He had just finished cooking for all the guests, as he did each day, and his face showed the fatigue of a day well spent.

"Just another mediocre day in paradise," he said, shaking my hand firmly, looking carefully at my face to see what sort of person fate had deposited at the doormat of the Balsam Mountain Inn this time. We walked down the hall to the dining room, our footsteps echoing sharply. The lady had no patience for useless decoration, soft furniture or frivolities. Only the polished surface of wood gleamed everywhere, and the dining room, where scores of simple tables and chairs stood, held the aura of past glories. Bob described the earliest days of the inn, dating from its opening in 1908 when a spur line from the railroad brought guests, eager refugees from the heat of Charleston and Atlanta and all over the South, there to spend the entire summer. Balls celebrated debutantes from Savannah and Chattanooga. Horse-drawn carriages rattled up the road to the inn, laden with steamer trunks filled with clothes to last until fall color. Guests danced under the stars, gazebos sheltered live orchestras, and everyone lived scenes out of Fitzgerald's *Great Gatsby*.

Day-long excursions on horse back visited a nearby mica mine. There were no locks on the doors of the inn, nor are there any to this day. Since the rooms had no closets, steamer trunks stood in the hallways outside the rooms. High ceilings and open doors provided natural air conditioning.

Bob spoke of the relationship between the inn and elements of nature. "Every April, when we open the hotel, we have to pry her from the mountains. There is grass growing up through the floor-boards and vines growing up the kitchen walls into the very cabinets and sinks. Bees swarm every year on the second story balcony. It is theirs. The guests are not allowed there. The corner column on the east side of the front porch is always full of honey. It is theirs also. The bats own the third floor. The guests are not allowed there either.

"Paul the gardener used bat guano from the hallway floor of the third story to grow the most productive garden in the region. Horticulturalists came from nearby colleges and universities to study his garden. He fed the guests fresh vegetables for years. At 73, he was the most eligible bachelor on the premises. He had a bungalow where he wined and dined the female guests that struck his fancy. One finally picked him off. We lost him.

"Every year when we connect the pipes from the spring on the mountain to the plumbing in the hotel, Sarah, the kids and I deploy ourselves throughout the hotel, and stand in the empty hallways, listening for the tinkle of water from broken pipes. I swear, I'll wake up at 3:00 a.m. and 'sense' a broken pipe in the west wall, and go to the very room. It's uncanny. Even if the plumbing is practically antebellum, we still have wonderful spring water here. In fact, the inn originally was called The Balsam Mountain Springs Hotel.

"And, oh, the local history that I've heard," Bob said. "Just the other day, I was talking to old Mr. Wells. He told me that he can still remember when the timber played out in these parts when he was a boy. The men who had worked for the timber company would come and knock on his father's door. They would ask for money for passage to Seattle, where there was work. He told me that his father never turned a man down, not even a stranger, and that he never failed to receive an envelope in the mail, paying him back. There is a town called Darrington, north of Seattle. It's full of people from North Carolina who left the Balsam area to work the timber on the west coast. Mr. Wells' father helped many of them get there. Makes you proud, doesn't it?"

"I came here as a youth, fell under the spell of these mountains and the life of the inn, gradually becoming more and more deeply involved. And now, if I leave, the inn will likely be closed." He spoke softly. "There is a grandfather clause that says if I leave, all the plumbing and wiring will have to be brought up to the new building code. It's not likely that anyone will spend that kind of money. She's very old, you know. Much of the foundation is made from solid chestnut."

Bob's wife Sarah spoke up. "Bob, you know that we've agreed that this is our last season. We're going to let nature run its course. Twenty-one years is enough."

"Yes." Bob sighed. It was after midnight. We had talked for more than four hours. Bob and I stood on the front porch. The moonlight showed the rounded forms of the hills, covered in forest. From the branches of the hardwoods came the voice of the mountains, the cicada. Their rattling insect calls were like waves in a stormy sea, first running randomly, then combining, finding a rhythm, forming a pulsing, irresistible chant, the very heartbeat of the Smokies.

"Just another mediocre night in paradise," Bob said. "Will I leave? I don't know anything for certain except this is the only place that has ever felt like 'home'."

Balsam Mountain Inn—"The Old Lady on the Hill."

The Splendid People

Above: This Tar Heel is having onions for dinner tonight.

Facing page, left: Fisherman mending his nets.
Right: Edward R. Murrow in London during World War II.

Fifteen years ago I was driving between Missoula, Montana and Lewiston, Idaho on Highway 12. I stopped at a time-worn hot springs resort amid dozens of small stone cottages. An old, silver-haired woman walked slowly out to greet me and, as we stood by the roaring Locksa River, she spoke softly in an unmistakable North Carolina accent. I asked her how she came to be here. She had come as a young bride and never had been back. I asked if she had found a home among the pragmatic, no-nonsense Westerners. Had she missed the Southerners? In one of the most eloquent, understated responses I will ever hear, she had very slowly, deliberately said, "This is splendid country." A sweeping gesture of her arms seemed to lead me gently away from my question. She would never again be among Southerners and I sensed a deep, almost pathetic longing, although she refused to comment on it—in true stoic Southern fashion.

Since that time, I have recognized my two separate worlds for what they are. One is the place of splendid country, where I can drink from the creeks and catch a skillet-full of brook trout from an irrigation ditch; the other is the place of splendid *people*, where I can tell my woes to a stranger in the grocery store and watch that stranger's face become lined with concern. I must have both.

Recently a friend from Montana came to visit me. He flew into Atlanta and hadn't been in the South for 30 minutes before he began to notice in everything from the "Southern Pride" carwash to the country and western group Alabama singing "Southern Born" on the radio, a sense of place that astonished him. Why is the South different? My Uncle Walker gave him the best explanation of it that I have heard. "In the North," he said, "the Puritans heavily influenced society. They outlawed bearbaiting, where pit bulls fought bears to the death, not out of concern for the animals, but because the people enjoyed it too much. Their grim outlook was perfect for the merchant mentality to evolve."

The shrewd Yankee traders became the best in the world, dealing in everything from slaves to whale oil. Salem, Massachusetts, so grimly single-minded, sometimes burned alive people who deviated from the Puritan mandates. As the stern Northerners searched for some new dimension of guilt, the Southerners, perhaps influenced by the "live-in-the-moment" attitude of the blacks, read Sir Walter Scott, searching for new visions of courtliness and chivalry. In the South, manners, flair and style always dominated. The supreme compliment to a Montana man might be that he is strong and unyielding before the elemenst—tough. In the South, the supreme compliment is to be called a gentleman. There is nothing beyond that.

From David Brinkley to Andy Griffith to the fiery conviction of Sam Ervin during the Watergate trial, North Carolina's native sons and daughters embody those traits the nation recognizes as the best, simplest and most honest. When North Carolinian Charles Kurault and his "On the Road" van tour tiny Texas crossroad towns and Idaho logging towns, his easy-going honesty and warmth win him admirers across the nation. He is living proof of the state's motto: "Esse Quam Videri" ("To Be Rather Than To Seem").

North Carolinians have not shied away from adversity. Greensboro-born Edward R. Murrow, born in abject poverty, became possibly America's greatest broadcast journalist. During War World II he flew in more than 40 combat missions over Germany, covering the war as a radio correspondent, and was known for his London rooftop broadcasts. Shy, melancholy Ed Murrow became the nation's highest-paid newsman, the king of broadcast news. Yet, when at the top of his profession, he made a speech that plagued his career for the rest of his days. Murrow questioned the ethics he saw deteriorating, not only in his profession, but within many facets of American life. He said:

"Let us have a little competition, not just in selling soap, cigarettes and automobiles. Just once in a while let us exalt the importance of ideas. It may be that the present system…can survive. Perhaps the money-making machine has some kind of built-in perpetual motion, but I do not think so.

"…our history will be what we make it. If we go on as we are, then history will take its revenge, and retribution will not limp in catching up with us."

North Carolina stands at a crossroads. It possesses an enviable quality of life, yet already over Charlotte and Asheville on windless days, a yellow haze of smog dirties the sky. Chapel Hill, Charlotte and Raleigh endure nightmarish traffic, and Chapel Hill has been transformed from a quiet, intellectual village into

JOHN RUCKER

North Carolina's native sons and daughters embody those traits the nation recognizes as the best, simplest and most honest.

Above: *North Carolina is a land of plenty in more ways than one.*
Right: *A library storyteller upholds the Southern oral tradition.*

Facing page: *A verdant, peaceful cemetery is a fitting symbol of North Carolinians' long history and family ties.*

CHIP HENDERSON PHOTOS BOTH PAGES

something very different. Greensboro's primary water supply, tiny Horsepen Creek, may not support three new 18-story office buildings as well as a swelling population.

In a 1987 poll by *Business Week*, North Carolina ranked first among corporate executives asked which state they would most likely consider for their next plant. With one of the lowest unionization rates in the country, 4.8 percent, and a strong work ethic, North Carolina may be on the verge of astounding growth. According to the *Greensboro News and Record*, North Carolina will become the fifth-fastest–growing state in the nation between the 1986 and 2010.

If Edward R. Murrow were alive and living in North Carolina today, and could see the rapid growth taking place—often with little regard for the environment where future generations will make their homes—he might make a passionate appeal for common sense. By changing only a few words from his speech of 30 years ago, he might urge us:

Let us have a little competition, not only in selling cigarettes, textiles and furniture. But just once in a while let us exalt the importance of living simply and the importance of the land, for these things are North Carolina's strength.

108

CHIP HENDERSON

CHIP HENDERSON

PAT COCCIADIFERRO

Left: *In Chimney Rock Park.*
Below, left: *A Blue Ridge farm.*
Below, right: *Ready for a family cruise.*

Facing page, top left: *A Durham Bulls baseball game.*
Bottom left: *Whitetail deer in the Smoky Mountains*
Right: *Mountain beauty.*

ROBERT MAUST

FOR FURTHER READING

Blythe, LeGette, and Charles Brockmann. *Hornet's Nest: The Story of Charlotte and Mecklenburg County*. Published for Public Library of Charlotte and Mecklenburg County by McNally of Charlotte, 1961.

Bradley, Jeff. *A Traveler's Guide to the Smoky Mountains Region*. Boston: The Harvard Common Press, 1985.

Cash, W.J. *The Mind of the South*. New York: Vintage Books, 1941, 1969.

Connor, R.D.W. *North Carolina: Rebuilding an Ancient Commonwealth 1584-1925*. Chicago & New York: The American Historical Society, Inc., 1929.

DeBlieu, Jan. *Hatteras Journal*. Golden, Colo.: Fulcrum Incorporated, 1987.

Kephart, Horace. *Our Southern Highlanders: A Narrative of Adventure in the Southern Appalachians and a Study of Life Among the Mountaineers*. Knoxville: University of Tennessee Press, 1913, 1976.

Lawson, John. *A New Voyage to Carolina*. Chapel Hill: University of North Carolina Press, 1967.

Lefler, Hugh Talmage, and Albert Ray Newsome. *The History of a Southern State*. Chapel Hill: University of North Carolina Press, 1973.

MacNeill, Ben Dixon. *The Hatterasman*. Winston-Salem: John F. Blair, 1958.

The North Carolina Guide. Chapel Hill: University of North Carolina Press, 1955.

Stick, David. *The Outer Banks of North Carolina, 1584-1958*. Chapel Hill: University of North Carolina Press, 1975.

Van Noppen, Ina W., and John J. Van Noppen. *Western North Carolina Since the Civil War*. Boone, N.C.: Appalachia Consortium Press, 1973.

William Byrd's Histories of the Dividing Line Betwixt Virginia and North Carolina, with Introduction and Notes by William K. Boyd. The North Carolina Historical Commission, 1929.

On the Outer Banks.